THE ESSENTIAL GUIDE TO

AMAZON ADVERTISING

By Thomas Herold

HOW TO ATTRACT MORE READERS AND SELL MORE BOOKS

THE ESSENTIAL GUIDE TO AMAZON ADVERTISING

HOW TO ATTRACT MORE READER AND SELL MORE BOOKS

Revision 1.23

Thomas Herold

bookadreport.com

Table of Contents

Copyright & Disclaimer

Introduction

This book focuses entirely on Amazon advertising, therefore let's start with a quick overview of this platform, and how it benefits you as an author. However, before I get to that, a little side note about this current edition.

It's still revision 1.0, and I wish I had planned a bit better ahead. I am once again surprised about my planning time and how fast the actual finishing date approached. I thought I had given myself plenty of time, but as you probably also wrote one or more book you know exactly what I am mean. My native language is German, and this first edition still contains some grammar errors. I apologize, and I will make it up by sending you a revised version once the second edition is ready.

Now that we have this out of the way lets dive into the large e-commerce business of Amazon.

Amazon has become the second Trillion Dollar company right after Apple. What started - just a decade ago - as a small online bookseller, has a few years later turned into the biggest bookstore, and is now the most significant e-commerce reseller. With 48 Million books listed (3.5 Million Kindle books), self-publishing on Amazon has become a breeze.

Due to Amazon's global scope and reach, it is also considered one of the most valuable brands worldwide.

The online retailer does not only lead regarding desktop retailing but has also taken to mobile commerce. Amazon Mobile is one of the most popular apps in the United States. The Amazon app via smartphone is also the second-most favorite purchase channel of Amazon buyers in the United States. Holiday sales in 2018 are expected to reach 50% of all online orders!

Amazon also offers Amazon Prime, an annual paid membership offering free two-day shipping in the United States as well as discounted one-day shipping rates, which current users regard as one of the key reasons for subscribing to the service. Amazon Prime has since opened to other countries and has also expanded to offer instant streaming of selected movies and television shows through Amazon Instant Video and music.

The average annual Amazon shopping expenditure of Amazon Prime members was found to be 1,300 U.S. dollars on the online shopping platform every year, compared to 700 U.S. dollars spending of non-Prime members. The most popular product categories of Amazon Prime shoppers in the United States were electronics and physical books, followed by e-books and personal care products.

Quick Facts About Amazon

During the most recently measured period, Amazon.com had almost 2.64 billion visits, up from 2.1 billion visits in February 2018. As of 2017, Amazon had 310 million active customers.[1]

- Half of all web shoppers will go to Amazon to search for a product.
- 51% of consumers planned to do all of their holiday shopping on Amazon.
- 64% of households subscribe to Amazon Prime
- 40% of all Amazon Prime members will spend over $1,000 a year on the site.
- 72% of all Amazon users will spend between $100 and $500 annually on the site.
- Over 100 million users use Amazon Prime globally.
- Amazon Users spent more than one-third of all their black Friday dollars on Amazon.
- Millenials tend to be the highest market as they are twice as likely to use Amazon as a Baby Boomer.[2]

As of 2017, there was a projected amount of approximately 88.8 million owners of e-readers in the United States, and that number is expected to increase to over 90 million by 2018.

Originally offered as a basic e-reader, the Kindle has strongly influenced e-book sales. The current Kindle Fire tablet range has transformed into a line of devices that also enable the consumption of media within the Amazon ecosystem. According to a study by PwC[3] The expected revenue for ebooks will grow from 2.31 billion in 2011 to 8.69 billion in 2018.

Audiobooks are on the Rise

While print books are still leading the way, audiobook consumption is notable because it is the one book format that is rising steadily. Currently, one in five US readers listens to audiobooks. The trend started in 2015, and there seems no reason why it will not continue to grow.

Smartphones are and will continue to be the most used device for reading ebooks and listening to audiobooks.

For you as an author, the future is apparent. Publish in all three formats to give your books the best chance of being read. Give readers the choice of versions, so they can buy your book in the form they prefer.

Your Earning Potential with Amazon

The new quarterly report from Data Guy and Hugh Howey's Author Earnings[4] spots 'more than 4,600 authors earning $25,000 or above from their sales on Amazon.com.' "1,340 authors are earning $100,000 per year or more from Amazon sales. Half of them are indies and Amazon-imprint authors."

"More than 50 percent of all traditionally-published book sales of any format in the US now happen on amazon.com. Roughly 85 percent of all non-traditionally published book sales of any format in the US also happen on Amazon.com.

"Roughly half of Amazon's daily ebook purchases are now going to indie authors."

"More than 4,600 authors earning $25,000 or above from their sales on Amazon.com. Forty percent of these are indie authors deriving at least half their income from self-published titles, while 35 percent are Big Five authors deriving the majority of their income from Big Five-published titles, and 22 percent are authors who derive most of their income from titles published by small- or medium-sized traditional publishers."

In Amazon's recent (2017) shareholder letter noted, there are more than a 1,000 authors who earn more than a $100,000 a year from their work published through Amazon.

"Today it's possible to be a full-time professional author, quietly earning $50,000+ a year - even six figures a year - without ever sending a query letter to anyone. On Amazon alone, the data shows over a thousand indie authors earning a full-time living right now with their self-published titles."

These numbers are great and encouraging...

Sadly, that also means your books will most likely collect dust without advertising! Fortunately, the rapid expansion of the Internet will soon add 2 billion more people that can buy your book with just one click.

If they know how to find it...

Advertising Books on Amazon Works

While advertisers now pay $20 or even more for one click on Google, promoting your books on Amazon is still possible with 5-10 cents per click. Even more important, people on Google search for information, people on Amazon search for products!

This means Amazon offers the highest potential to turn book searches into book sales.

In this essential advertising guide, you will learn every single detail of how to use Amazons book advertising service to attract more readers and sell more books.

- How to find the best keywords in less than 15 minutes
- Includes a 70% discount code for the best keyword research tool
- How to write successful, targeted ad copies
- Five KDP secrets Amazon keeps hidden from you
- How to optimize your campaign for optimum ROI
- How to set up Sponsored Product Ads and Product Display Ads
- Three ad optimization techniques you must use
- Free tool to get hundreds of relevant keywords
- How to use GoodReads to build your keyword list
- How to split test and find the best performing ad
- The best tool to track your ads and improve performance

Start Selling More Books on Amazon

Running ads on Amazon is not a set and forget tactic - I wish it were. For your ads to perform up to their potential, you have to go in and nurture your keyword list to stay up to date with the latest search trends for books.

Advertising on Amazon with KDP is complex, and if you have no experience how it works, you will waste your money, and most likely give up soon.

After reading this book, you will be able to create targeted ads, track performance, make adjustments, sell more books and increase your income.

With a little patience, you may even make a living by doing what you love - writing books.

Chapter I - How Does Amazon Book Advertising Work?

Book Market Overview - Statistics & Facts

Statista offers some remarkable statistics & facts about the U.S. book publishing market, which gives you some interesting insights. In case you get quickly bored by facts skip this chapter.

The revenue from the global book publishing market is forecast to slightly increase in the coming years, growing from around 113 billion U.S. dollars in 2015 to about 123 billion U.S. dollars by 2020.[5]

Projections for the book publishing industry in the U.S. are optimistic. Revenue from this industry in the U.S. is projected to reach to nearly 44 billion U.S. dollars in 2020, a significant increase from 2016. About 2.7 billion books were sold in the U.S. in 2015, a figure that has remained fairly consistent in the last few years.

E-books have been gaining pace in the book industry in the U.S. About 73 percent of publishers and authors had published their books digitally in the U.S. in 2015, and nearly 80 percent stated planning to publish e-books in 2016. Despite the rising popularity of e-books in the U.S. among publishers, forecasts show that the number of e-books readers is expected to slightly drop in the coming years. In 2015, there were 92.64 million people reading e-books in the country. By 2021, this figure is projected to drop to 88.45 million.

Audiobooks Gain Popularity

I love listening to books and other things when I drive or even sometimes to chill out in the evening. Somehow it takes less attention than reading a book. By the way, publishing an audiobook is easier than you think. I will go into this topic at the end of this book.

Audiobooks, which first gained popularity in the consumer market in the cassette tape and CD era, are back in the digital media era. The number of audiobook published in the U.S. increased dramatically in the last few years, going from about 7,200 published titles in 2011 to more than 35,500 published titles in 2015. Self-help/spirituality audiobooks are particularly popular in the U.S., as 35 percent of audiobook listeners in the U.S. stated preferring this audiobook genre.

Despite the rise of digital book formats, printed books still have their space in the market. Unit sales of published books in the U.S. saw a decline from 2008 until 2012, reaching the lowest figure of the last decade that year. After 2012, sales of printed books started to gain momentum, and have slightly increased up until 2015. Sales figures aside, published books are still the preferred format of 65 percent of book readers in the U.S.

How Do People Read?

About 73 percent of book readers in the U.S. said they read books in any format. The average American aged 18 to 49 reads 12 books per year, while the average number of books read by 65 or older Americans is slightly higher – a total of 13 books per year. Some 23 percent of respondents in a 2017 survey stated that they read print books and e-books equally, while 20 percent said that they read more e-books.

Mystery, thriller and crime genre is the leading book genre in the U.S., as nearly half of American consumers prefer this genre. About 33 percent of them stated history was their favorite book genre, and 31 percent of Americans said biographies and memoir was their preferred type of book.

What Do People Read?

During a survey, 27 percent of respondents stated they had read a romance in the year leading up to the study. The most popular genre was mystery, thriller and crime books, which 47 percent of respondents had admitted to reading in the past year.

A similar trend can be seen amongst e-book readers, as 50 percent of respondents in a recent survey stated that mystery/thriller books were their favorite genre of e-books. The genre which has experienced the most significant sales growth in the last few years is the romantic comedy genre, which has recorded sales growth of 357 percent.

Book Genres That Make the Most Money

Based on the facts above this is also where the most money flows.

1. *Romance/Erotica - $1.44 billion* - From the success of the Fifty Shades of Grey trilogy and the number of novels written by people like Danielle Steele, there's no surprise that romance and erotica are #1.

2. *Crime/Mystery* - $728.2 million - There's nothing like the thrill from a mystery novel. The suspense is intriguing enough that it keeps you on board. It's all about the build-up, the surprises, even the letdowns. Crime and mystery stories are so wild and fascinating, but also seem plausible.

3. *Religious/Inspirational* - $720 million - Things may be going great but you may need a little push. Everyone can use some inspiration. From how-to books, holy texts, and even memoirs, inspirational and religious texts.

4. *Science Fiction/Fantasy* - $590.2 million - Dragons, elves, witches, robots, the possibilities are endless. We love escaping into a fictional land. There's nothing that people can't achieve through magic, or extraordinary circumstances in this genre.

5. *Horror - $79.6 million* - Horror has earned its place on this list. If you think of Stephen King and the ways his work has been adapted to screen, or old horror like Dracula and Frankenstein, there are endless stories that people love. [6]

Please understand that the data above reflects the whole book market and not only the Kindle market.

Most Competitive Kindle Category Rankings

TCK Publishing did a great research on the Kindle market. Which categories can give you the most sales possible on Amazon Kindle? Here are the first 10 of the list. You will find the complete list of 100 entries on their website.

1. Romance -> Contemporary
2. Literature & Fiction -> Contemporary Fiction -> Women
3. Romance -> New Adult & College
4. Literature & Fiction -> Contemporary Fiction -> Romance
5. Literature & Fiction -> Women -> Romance
6. Literature & Fiction -> Genre Fiction -> Coming of Age
7. Romance -> Mystery & Suspense -> Suspense
8. Science Fiction & Fantasy -> Fantasy -> Paranormal & Urban
9. Literature & Fiction -> Genre Fiction -> Erotica
10. Literature & Fiction -> Women -> Mystery, Thriller & Suspense -> Women Sleuths

You might have noticed that the list is dominated by fiction categories. There are only 12 non-fiction categories out of the Top 100 most competitive categories on Amazon Kindle, and the Top 21 are all fiction!

The #1 most competitive nonfiction list is Biographies & Memoirs -> Memoirs, which is dominated by celebrity memoirs like Sheryl Sandberg's Lean In.

What you might also notice if you start browsing these categories on Amazon is that many of the top books in these competitive categories are by self-published and independently published authors. The big publishers aren't dominating like they used to.

Least Competitive Kindle Category Rankings

TCK Publishing also published a list of the 100 least competitive categories. Here they go with just showing you the first 10. If you want to see the complete list of 100 please visit their website.

1. Nonfiction -> Science -> Experiments, Instruments & Measurement -> Microscopes & Microsocopy
2. Nonfiction -> Business & Money -> Taxation -> Corporate
3. Business & Money -> Taxation -> Corporate
4. Science -> Experiments, Instruments & Measurement -> Microscopes & Microsocopy
5. Professional & Technical -> Engineering -> Civil -> Hydrology
6. Nonfiction -> Professional & Technical -> Engineering -> Civil -> Hydrology
7. Nonfiction -> Science -> Experiments, Instruments & Measurement -> Weights & Measures
8. Science -> Experiments, Instruments & Measurement -> Weights & Measures
9. Nonfiction -> Crafts, Hobbies & Home -> How-to & Home Improvements -> Masonry
10. Crafts, Hobbies & Home -> How-to & Home Improvements -> Masonry

One big thing you can learn from this list is that most of the least competitive bestseller lists on Amazon are for nonfiction. The only fiction categories on this list are children's ebooks. Children's ebooks are a very tiny market compared to major fiction genres like romance, science fiction, fantasy, thriller, suspense, mystery, etc.

What People Read Depends on Their Age

While it is mostly believed that book reading is a vanishing pastime, particularly among Millennials, surveys among consumers in the U.S. have shown the opposite. The share of book readers in the U.S. has varied from 72 percent to 79 percent between 2011 and 2016.

In regards to age of book readers in the country, a 2016 survey shows about 80 percent of respondents between the ages of 18 to 29 had read at least one book in the previous 12 months, the highest share amongst all age groups. About 73 percent of the respondents aged between 30 to 49 years old said they read at least one book in the last 12 months.

The share among respondents between 50 and 64 years old stood at 70 percent, whereas 67 percent of respondents aged 65 plus stated reading book during the time measured. In terms of education level, book readers in the U.S. are more likely to have a college degree, or at least some college education – 86 percent and 81 percent respectively.

Women in the U.S. read slightly more than men; 68 percent of male respondents started reading at least one book in the previous 12 months, against 77 percent of female respondents that said the same.

Despite the rise of digital platforms and the rising popularity of e-reading devices such as Kindle, Kobo and others, printed books still remain the most popular book format in the U.S., as 65 percent of Americans stated preference for printed books in 2016.

E-books were consumed by 28 percent of respondents in 2016, whereas audio books were listened by 14 percent of the respondents. Millennials accounted for the largest share of printed book readers in the U.S. – 72 percent as of 2016.

For further stats and more details on the book market, please check the Resource section at the end of this book.

People Shift Away From Kindle Devices

Devices such as Kindle, Nook, and Kobo are all suffering from a rapid drop off in sales, yet readers are still buying and reading e-books more than ever. In 2010, Amazon's Kindle accounted for 62.8 percent of all e-reader shipments worldwide. [7]

This number has dropped since then as other readers are available, however the major reason is the shift away from Kindle to other devices like mobil phones and tablets.

One of the main problems is that devices have failed to develop in any major technical form since their introduction in 2008. If you own a Kindle from 2009, you will know that it is almost exactly the same as the current model. In fact, I believe my old Kindle is better, as it came with audio, which has been removed from later models.

In a market study[8] from 2015 Some 19% of adults report owning an e-reader – a handheld device such as a Kindle or Nook primarily used for reading e-books. This is a sizable drop from early 2014, when 32% of adults owned this type of device. Ownership of e-readers is somewhat more common among women (22%) than men (15%).

The rise of the smartphone has had a major social, political and cultural impact. It has changed the way people reach their friends, obtain data and media, and share their lives. Fully 68% of adults now have a smartphone, nearly double the share that Pew Research Center measured in its first survey on smartphone ownership in mid-2011. At that point, 35% of adults had smartphones.

Close to Half of Americans own a Tablet

The share of Americans who own a tablet computer has risen tenfold since 2010. Today, 45% of U.S. adults own a tablet – a substantial increase since Pew Research Center began measuring tablet ownership in 2010. Then, only 4% of adults in the U.S. were tablet owners. Ownership, however, is statistically the same as it was in 2014.

The Use of Desktop or Laptop Computers

Ownership for traditional computers has remained stable. Some 73% of U.S. adults own a desktop or laptop computer. This figure has fluctuated a bit in Pew Research findings over the years, but the 2015 finding is roughly similar to computer ownership levels of a decade ago – though slightly down from a high in 2012, when 80% of Americans said they had a desktop or laptop.

Sales of Audiobooks Are Soaring

One medium that bridges the gap between the traditional book market and new forms of technology is the audiobook. Sales revenues have soared in this area, more than doubling between 2010 and 2016. This growing demand for audiobooks can be seen in the fact that the number of audiobook titles published in the United States has grown from approximately 6,200 to over 50,00 in the same time frame. [9]

One of the major selling points of audiobooks is the capacity for on-the-go listening, allowing consumers to listen to their favorite books in the car, on the commute to work, or while on a run. However, some 52 percent of consumers also listen to audiobooks on a desktop or laptop, suggesting that there is also a big demand for audiobooks in the home.

According to a survey, 57 percent of respondents browse through a library or a library's website to find information about new audiobooks and 56 percent of consumers consult their local bookstores. Whilst some claim that audiobooks and e-books may spell the end for conventional book stores and libraries, it seems that they are, in fact, contributing to their growth. In 2017, approximately 68 million audiobooks were borrowed from libraries and schools in the United States, along with 155 million e-books.

However, whilst the evidence suggests that audiobooks are increasing in popularity in the United States, the reality is that conventional print books still remain the most popular way to read a book.

In the past audiobooks gained popularity in cassette tape and CD formats but more recently a shift into the digital media territory has been detected. Downloadable audiobooks can be beneficial for both producers and users as they do not require large production costs, storage inventory, physical packaging, or transportation.

The primary market for audiobooks is found in well-educated adults who have a preference for books over television. Among those surveyed in the United States in January 2014, 21 percent of college graduates claimed to have listened to an audiobook in the past 12 months, as opposed to only 10 percent who have a high school education or less.

As of 2013 however the audiobook was by no means dominating the book industry in the United States. In 2013, only 14 percent of respondents surveyed stated listening to an audiobook at least once in the past 12 months, whereas 69 percent claimed to have read at least one print book.

The convenience of audiobooks allows its users to multi-task, ideal for an ever increasingly on-the-go lifestyle. In 2012, the political commentator Bill O'Reilly's "Killing Kennedy" and "Killing Lincoln" which are books known for their riveting narratives of historical assassinations proved most popular with audiobook consumers as they topped the audiobook charts, selling 58,101 units and 52,696 units respectively.

Leading audiobook genres in the United States in 2017

Leading audiobook genres in the United States in 2017, by units sold (in millions)[10].

1. Literature & Fiction 2.75
2. Fiction & Literature 2.18
3. Mystery, Thriller & Suspense 1.6
4. Science Fiction & Fantasy 1.38
5. Romance 1.33

6. Business & Money 1
7. Children's Books 0.97
8. Biographies & Memoirs 0.96
9. Mysteries & Thrillers 0.85
10. Fantasy 0.76

Takeaway from this Book Market Overview

While print books are still leading the way, audiobook consumption is rising steadily. Currently, every fifth reading person in the US listens to audiobooks. Smartphones are and will continue to be the most used device for reading ebooks and listening to audiobooks.

Publish in all three formats to give your books the best chance of being read. Give readers the choice of versions, so they can buy your book in the form they prefer. Use the simple setup option on Amazon to turn your ebook into a Paperback or Hardcover version. Because of the initial setup costs, the Paperback version offers you a better revenue - based on the number of sales - than the Hardcover version.

Also, you may not know that you can now publish your book in audio form on Audible, which is owned by Amazon, for zero upfront cost! A revenue sharing model makes this possible.

The Basics on Book Advertising with Amazon

Book advertising on Amazon works in similar ways than advertising with Google Ads. It's a bidding and auction system that grants the highest bidder a place for their ad next to a book.

Sponsored books are mostly keyword-targeted ads that promote your listings and appear in search results and on book product detail pages on Amazon. You select your book to advertise and choose your keywords or let Amazon target your ads with automatic targeting. You control how much you want to spend on your bids and budgets and can measure your ads' performance. A bit more about measuring ad performance in a later chapter, which is essential to your success with ads.

Putting your ad in front of people who are already looking for a book to buy is the perfect opportunity for you as an author. People don't go to Facebook to buy books, they go to Amazon, and this is why Amazon ads are better for authors than any other type of book advertising.

Besides that, while Amazon ads are perfect for launching a new book, it's also an effective way to refresh sales of an older book. Whether you have old books that are dead or have a brand new book coming out, advertising with Amazon Marketing Services can help you sell more books and bring in more cash.

With targeted Amazon ads, you should see continuous sales, which increases your ranking in your chosen categories. With higher category ranking, you will gain more exposure, more readers, and generate more sales.

There are currently two different ad types available...

Sponsored Product Ads

They appear below Amazon search results and below the fold on product (book) pages. Sponsored Product ads can be targeted by keyword or can use auto-targeting. They deliver relevant ads in search results based on keyword searches. When clicked, the ad sends shoppers directly to your book's detail page from their search.

Ads appear below search results, and below the fold on product detail pages.

Product Display Ads

They appear on related product detail pages and can appear on the Kindle reader screensaver and home screen. Product Display ads can be targeted by book genre or relevant products. They deliver interest or product-targeted ads to customers on detail pages and Kindle E-readers, where eligible. When clicked, the ad redirects shoppers directly to your detail page.

Ads appear on related product detail pages, on Kindle E-reader screensaver and home screen for eligible ads.

Amazon Book Ads - Requirements & Legal Aspects

Currently, you can only run ads on Amazon.com. You can advertise books written in languages other than English, but all language in the ad must match the language of the Amazon site where the ad's running.

For example, if you want to advertise a book written in Japanese on Amazon.com, the ad must be in English. Also, book titles must clearly state if the book isn't in the language of the Amazon site where the ad's running.

Customers who click your ad will be taken to your book's product detail page, and a strong book detail page can help convert the click into a sale. Here are a few guidelines that will help you with your first ads.

Make sure your detail page has:

- An accurate, descriptive title
- High-quality images
- Relevant and useful information
- Support for any claims made in your ads
- Title, Headline, and Custom Text (where available)

The following are prohibited on Title, Headline, and Custom Text:

- Unnecessary information
- Profanity, including obfuscated or censored profanity
- Special characters or symbols, including legal symbols (for example, ©)
- Email addresses or full or partial website URLs
- Sentences ending with article words (e.g., "Sample Book, The")
- Sentences with multiple punctuation marks
- Pricing messages
- Emotionally draining or depressing messages
- Customer reviews, unless the specific review is contained in the book description on the detail page
- Third-party customer reviews or rating scores, third-party editorial reviews are acceptable
- References to the Amazon rating score
- References or acronyms related to certain sexual practices (such as BDSM, Dom, Sub or MMF)
- Phrases with an inappropriate or offensive double meaning
- References alluding to an incestualized romantic relationship

- Overly forceful phrases or exclamation points (e.g. "Don't miss out!", "HURRY - SAVE NOW")
- Special offers, promotions or contests
- References to Kindle Unlimited (KU) or statements such as "Free on Kindle"

Please also know that ad copies in ALL CAPS are not allowed. Capitalization is only acceptable where the book cover or title on the detail page is formatted in the same way, or the word is a well-known abbreviation such as DIY (do it yourself) or YA (young adult).

Be Careful with Claims and Amazon Brand Usage

If the ad refers to another title, it cannot imply surpassing the other book or its writer (for example, we would not approve "more suspenseful than [Other Book Title]")

Claims, awards, or accolades used in the headline or custom text must be supported on the product detail page or within the ad with the source and date of the designation. For example, a claim such as "Best Seller in the US" in the headline would require "Best Seller in the US, NY Times, March 2017" on the product detail page.

Examples of claims, awards, or accolades which require substantiation include best-selling books, bestselling series, bestselling author, award-winning book, and award-winning author.

Amazon Customer Reviews are acceptable, only if it is clear in the ad that it is an Amazon Customer Review and the review is contained in the book description or editorial review section on the detail page. Unpaid third-party editorial reviews are acceptable if they are attributed to the original source.

Your ad text should not contain third-party customer reviews, star ratings or rating scores. Also, please know that headline and custom text that mentions the name Amazon must comply with Brand Usage Guidelines and does not include the Amazon logo.

Unacceptable Books and Ad Content

All advertising content must be appropriate for a general audience, conform to Amazon's Creative Acceptance Policies, and comply with all laws, rules, and regulations that apply to the advertiser, the advertising content, and any location where the advertisements may appear.

As part of amazons commitment to provide the highest quality customer experience, it is their policy not to display ads containing or relating to certain products, services, or content that violates Amazon's Creative Acceptance Policies.

Acceptable For All Ads

- Works of fiction that have political themes.
- Non-fiction books about politics in general or political science.
- Non-fiction books about religion in general
- Fiction books with religious themes

In most cases you will never have a problem with any of Amazon ad requirements or policies. My ads got rejected a few times, but in every case it was due to misspelling. From thousands of keywords I selected I never had any rejections. Just know that you can't use the word ‚Kindle‘.

You can find more details in the FAQ section of Kindle Direct Publishing. Also please check the resource section of this book to get more information on this topic.

https://kdp.amazon.com/en_US/help/topic/G201499010#faq

Why I Almost Gave Up on Amazon Advertising

When I started in 2017 with my first ad on Amazon I had very high expectations. I was reading a lot of articles from other authors claiming how simple and easy it was to advertise a book on Amazon.

Advertising on Amazon is easy, however, making a profit on book sales is another story. So, I started out creating my first ad. I wrote the ad copy, collected a few keywords that I thought would be relevant to my readers, and decided on bidding 20 cents per keyword.

Guess what happened?

Not much - after about two days I got a few hundred impressions. A few days later another few hundred impressions more. I thought this is very cumbersome.

First realization - I may not have enough keywords. So, I was reading articles on how to collect keywords and found a few tips and tricks here and there. I was excited and thought that this was going to push my impressions high up.

Guess what happened?

A few days later I checked my impressions, and my face got bored by the numbers. Not much had changed - I got a few hundred impressions more, but not even one click. How could that be with millions of people looking for books on Amazon? What was I doing wrong?

Reading more articles about keywords and advertising on Amazon to the rescue. I realized that it's maybe not the number of keywords, more like the right ones. So, I paused a few hundred keywords that got no impressions and added a few more keywords that I thought would be targeted to my audience.

Now, what you think happened this time?

Nothing! I hit the point where I got frustrated and terminated that ad. That was the end of the rope, and my idea about selling more of my books on Amazon died right there.

After a month I had gathered new energy and had written a few more articles from authors claiming how well their books are selling through Amazon with the help of advertising. I learned that the right keywords are essential and bid testing is crucial to success.

So, with new gathered steam I set up a new ad with fewer, targeted keywords and this time I was bold and set the bid price to 40 cents. If I only could see ahead what was coming down the pipe.

Finally, something surprising happened...

I checked the next day, and my ad got already over a thousand impressions. But what was that click counter showing - nothing! I waited another few days, and finally, the first clicks arrived. Not too bad, I thought - it looks like it's working now.

A jump ahead and it's ten days later. My ad got several thousand impressions and 18 clicks, which cost me around five dollars. I had the sales price of my book set to $7.95 and a bit more than five dollars was what I earned from one sale.

Let's wait I said to myself and left the ad running for a month, which I did. After five weeks my spending on this campaign had reached around $21 dollar, and I had not one sale. At this point, I quit, and I assume many other authors did as well.

Of course, I pulled myself out of the dump, and a year later I started another attempt where I finally saw the light of the tunnel. For almost another year I focused on making advertising on Amazon a success.

I wished I had the knowledge and experience when I was starting. However, now you don't have to put yourself to the slump, and when you are finished reading this book, you have set your footprints toward succeeding with Amazon book advertising.

I did not write about my previous advertising mistakes to discourage you. The intention was to show you what may happen when you start driving a car without acquiring the driver license.

Setting Up Your Amazon Marketing Account

If you already have an Amazon account sign in to Kindle Direct Publishing (KDP) with your existing Amazon username and password. You can skip the rest of this chapter.

If you don't have an Amazon account go to KDP and click "Sign up." Then click "Create your KDP account" and enter your name, email address, and a secure password. Once you've created your account, you'll need to enter author, payment, and tax information.

Author/Publisher Information

Enter your first and last name or the name of your publishing company and the mailing address you want Amazon to use for tax reporting purposes and royalty payments.

Note: Don't enter your pen name here. This matters because Amazon issue your payments and tax forms under the same name. If you want to use a pen name, enter it when you're setting up your book details.

How Do You Get Paid?

When setting up your account, you'll need to provide details for receiving royalty payments. Available payment methods (direct deposit, wire transfer or check) are based on the location of your bank.

Direct deposit, also known as electronic funds transfer (EFT), has no minimum payment threshold, and it's the fastest, most secure and environmentally friendly way to receive your royalty payments.

You'll be paid in full approximately 60 days after the end of every month for all your sales, regardless of the amount, and in your local currency.

KDP pays royalties every month, approximately 60 days after the end of the month in which they were earned. For example, you'll be paid in October for royalties earned in August, as long as they meet the minimum threshold. You'll receive separate royalty payments for each Amazon marketplace in which you have chosen to distribute your title.

Available payment methods (direct deposit, wire transfer, or check) are based on the location of your bank. Your bank may have fees associated with some payments. Please contact your bank to verify fees associated with receiving payments.

Direct deposit payments do not have a threshold!

Using the Direct Deposit Option

Choosing direct deposit, also known as electronic funds transfer (EFT), as a payment method allows you to receive your earned royalties without a minimum threshold before the funds are released to you; in a more secure and environmentally friendly way than paper checks; and in your local currency. There's also a handling fee of $8/£8/€8 per check payment to authors who reside in the US, UK, or EU countries where we offer direct deposit.

To avoid the handling fee, sign up for direct deposit!

After you switch to direct deposit, the change will take effect immediately. You'll be paid in full for all of your sales, regardless of the amount, in your local currency approximately 60 days after the end of the month in which the royalties accrued.

Provide Your Tax Information

U.S. tax regulations require Amazon to collect information about your tax status under U.S. law with the online tax interview on your KDP Account page. Amazon must receive and validate your tax information before you can update existing books or publish new books in the Kindle store.

The tax interview guides you step-by-step through gathering all the information required to establish your tax identity. Tax withholding and specific requirements vary depending on whether you're located in the U.S. or another country.

These are just the basics. For more detailed information please refer to the Kindle Direct Publishing FAQ section located here:

https://kdp.amazon.com/en_US/help/topic/G200634350

Chapter 2 - Creating Your First Ad

Write & Publish Your First Ad

In this chapter, you will write your first ad and get it approved. We will cover the details of all ad campaign aspects later. This will give you an overview of what needs to be done, and what's the difference between the two available ad campaign options.

Go to your Amazon advertise campaign dashboard and click on the ‚New campaign' button. You will see two boxes. One of them is the ‚Sponsored Products' option, and the other is the ‚Product Display Ad' option. When you take a closer look at the pictures, you will see an orange section. This section gives you an overview where your ad on the book description page shows up.

Click the ‚Continue' button below the ‚Sponsored Products' section. The first section you will see now covers the Settings. Start by changing the default campaign name to something more meaningful. For example a short version of your book title, then a hyphen and maybe a date or the words ‚First Test'. You could also include the first two letters of this ad option (e.g. SP). Your name could look like this: My Book Title - SP - First Test.

It's crucial that you change the name of your campaign as Amazon does not allow you to do this after you submitted it for review.

Leave the start date and the end date as it is. It means the ad should start running today and has no end date. No end date means it will run as long as you either pause it or terminate it.

Add your daily budget (e.g. $10). No worries here - you will not spend $10 per day. This number is the maximum amount you are willing to pay per day on this ad. To spend $10, you need to hit a very broad market and bid a high amount of money. I never had an ad even coming close to this. Amazon states that most campaigns with a budget of over $5.00 run throughout the day.

Next is the targeting option. You can choose between automatic targeting and manual targeting. If you want automatic targeting, then Amazon targets your ads to all relevant customer searches based on your product information. Amazons algorithm collects and uses relevant keywords for all selected products.

If you choose manual targeting, then you add your own keywords or phrases to your campaign based on your book's content, genre, and similar authors. You can also use suggested keywords from the ad builder. Manual targeting allows you to edit your keywords after adding them.

Please choose manual targeting for now. We will later discuss in details the various options with its purpose and expected results.

The next section is named 'Ad format', and here you select Custom text ad. Now scroll further down, and you will see the next section where you can choose the book you want to advertise. You can promote your Kindle or your Paperback version of your book. For your first ad campaign, please find your Kindle version and select it.

Moving on, the next section is called Keywords and bids. The first box is labeled default keyword bit and already contains a bid. Please use 0.21 cents right now - you can later adjust this number. After that, you will see a checkbox where you can allow Amazon to change the bid price automatically by 50%. Right now please leave this box unchecked.

Below that section, you will see a table that contains already some keywords based on your book title and book description. Go through all of them and kit the Add button on the right side for keyword suggestion that contains at least two words. Do not add any keywords which include just one word. You don't want to go to broad with your first campaign. You can add and pause keywords after your ad is approved and live.

After you have done this, you get to the next section, where you can add negative keywords.

What's that? Negative keywords prevent your ads from displaying when a shopper's search terms match your negative keywords. You can exclude irrelevant searches, reducing your advertising cost. I will explain this in detail later. For now, leave this box empty as it is.

Scroll further down, and you get to the last section of your first ad campaign setup. It wasn't that difficult until here, right? You have up to 150 characters to add your ad text. Be careful here, as you can't change this later on. If you want to change the ad text, you need to make a copy and retire the original!

Think about a sentence or two that could entice your reader to be interested in your book. If you have a novel, you want o make the reader curious without giving away to much of the story. If you have a non-fiction book point out the main benefit, the reader gets from your book.

After you have filled in your book description take a look at the preview section of your book in the box below. Some browsers may have difficulty showing you the preview! Your ad may look slightly different than what you see in this preview as Amazon continually test new features to determine which characteristics drive ad performance.

Hit the orange ,Launch campaign' button on the right bottom. Congratulations! You just wrote your first book ad.

What happens next?

Most likely your new ad will be approved in about one day. If you made any spelling mistakes your ad may be rejected, and you will get an email with some hints to where the problem lies. Your ad will appear then in draft mode. Correct the problem and submit it again.

What are Sponsored Product Ads?

Let's dive a bit deeper and get into the two different ad types that Amazon provides for book advertising. If you have an Amazon seller account, you have a third option for advertising. This other ad type is called '#Headline Ads'. However, it's not available for KDP book advertisement at this time.

Sponsored Product ads are targeted by keywords, appearing within search results and on product detail pages across desktop and mobile. With a simple campaign creation process, the Sponsored Product ads are the recommended way to get you started advertising on Amazon.

By using your own keywords you are entirely in charge of your ad exposure and results. Choosing keywords means you can target your ad to a very narrow niche or go broad. You can cover an entire segment of your targeted book market with just one ad. Amazon allows you to add up to 1000 keywords for one ad. I do not recommend this approach until you know exactly what you do.

Why?

Because it's very hard to maintain, improve and to track. My recommendation is to use less than 100 keywords per campaign. I have a separate chapter on how to find and use keywords effectively.

Manual or Automatic Targeting

This ad format gives you two options to use keywords - your own or the ones Amazon decides. The manual keyword option comes with an extra bid adjustment choice -

Bid+. It's s feature that increases the opportunity for your ads to show in the top of search results. When Bid+ is turned on, Amazon increases the default bid for your ads by up to 50% when they compete for the top of search results location (provided they are eligible to show there).

Bid+ Example

If your default bid is $0.50, Bid+ can raise your bid as high as $0.75 to compete for impressions at the top of search results. You can turn on Bid+ for any manually targeted campaign. Bid+ is only available for the top of search results location, and can only be turned on for manually targeted campaigns. The daily budget will remain as you set it, regardless of Bid+.

You can turn Bid+ on and off in your Campaign Settings Manager. To get started, go to the Campaign Settings tab on your dashboard and enable once your campaign is active.

I have not tested this feature enough to give you meaningful data. However, I will update this book once there is a significant amount of data to make a recommendation.

If you select automated targeting, Amazon targets your ads to all relevant customer searches based on your product information. Their algorithm collects and uses relevant keywords for all selected products.

This is a very powerful feature; however, I do not recommend it when you are just getting started with advertising on Amazon. I only have a few of these automatic ads running, and it took a while until they began to perform well.

The reason for this is the internal algorithm that Amazon uses. When your automated targeted ad is new, Amazon has no historical data, and your ad will appear most likely randomly, but within your genre. Remember Amazon only uses your book title and description to match your ad with potential buyers.

However, after your ad runs for a month or two, you will see improvements in your ACoS column. This means you need more patience with this targeted option.

My two automated targeting ads are generating almost 1/3 of my revenue. They have high numbers of impression and also high click rates, but it took a while to get there.

I recommend you start with Sponsored Product ads, get yourself familiar with its performance, and also experiment with keyword groups and bidding before you go to automated targeting.

Summary - Sponsored Products (eBook and Paperback)

- Delivers relevant ads in Amazon search results based on keyword searches
- When clicked, the ad sends customers directly to your book's detail page
- Increase visibility in search results and detail pages with keyword-targeted ads
- Target by keyword, using automatic, suggested or custom keywords
- Five keyword match types to help you reach the right readers: broad, phrase, exact, negative phrase, negative exact
- Your ad appears within and below search results at top, middle, and bottom of product detail pages
- You control your spend by setting your bids and daily budget
- You're only charged when customers click on your ad
- The minimum average daily budget is $1
- Run campaign continuously or choose a custom date range

What are Product Display Ads?

Product Display ads are a completely different beast of campaign ad, because they work entirely without keywords. There are two targeting options available:

By Product
Product-targeted ads appear on Amazon when a reader browses for the products you select to target and similar products. Targeting by-product may yield fewer impressions as they are specific to the selected products. Please note product-targeted ads are not currently shown on Kindle E-readers.

When you choose this product based ad option you can select between two targeting options:

- Target Specific Products
- Target Related Categories

For targeting specific products you choose from a list of products which you can find by using keywords, product name, UPC or ASIN. Beneath your selected products you will find a checkbox that automatically extends your reach to include related products, such as those frequently bought with your book. Amazon recommends you keep this box checked. Unchecking this box greatly reduces your campaign's potential number of impressions.

I have not experimented with that option yet, and can't give you any advice. If you have some experience with it, please drop me a note.

To target related categories works by selecting one or more categories from the available categories Amazon provides. Depending on your book genre this could be limited to only one or two categories. For my book ‚The Money Deception‘ I only get to choose the preselected category ‚Economics‘.

Product targeting ads need more time to get running. You need to be patient. Allow at least ten days until you make any changes in the bid amount.

By Interest

Interest-targeted ads appear on Kindle E-readers and Amazon readers interested in the categories you select. Targeting by interest may yield more impressions as you are casting a wider net.

Choosing this option allows you to select from all available categories! Here, you can experiment with different categories. Something that is not possible with the product targeting option. However, this ad type has another feature, which makes it very likely you won't see a lot of sales, but lots of clicks.

Using interest targeting Amazon includes your ad on Kindle home screens. Yes, that's the people who have paid less money for their Kindle, and in return, Amazon puts an advertisement on the home screen. Yes, we are talking about your ad!

What do you think have people in common that allow advertising on their reading device for the exchange of saving $20-30? I think that's people with very little money in their pocket. A majority of these people may not be very well educated, and therefore only interested in books with entertainment value.

I had tested a series of ads with my book ‚The Money Deception‘, which may appeal to a wider audience due to to the fact of having ‚money‘ in the title. All four ads I tested with a price point of $7.95 failed miserably.

However, after testing it with a price tag of $2.99 I had a few sales and broke even. I assume that the price point is critical and if you do a book launch with $0.99-$2.99 you may be successful with it.

Always experiment once you have established your ads successfully and you are making a profit. Product display ads may also work very well in conjunctions with any other advertising promotion.

So, until you have the latest erotic or horror thriller at a bargain price, please do yourself a favor and stay away from this ad type - at least in the beginning.

Product Display ads (eBook only)

- Delivers interest or product-targeted ads on detail pages and Kindle E-readers, where eligible
- When clicked, the ad can redirect customers to your book's detail page
- Build name recognition and title awareness with interest and product-targeted ads on detail pages
- Target by book genre
- Target by related or relevant products, even outside of books
- Your ad appears on related product detail pages and/or on Kindle E-reader screensaver and home screen for eligible ads
- You control your spend by setting your bids and total campaign budget
- You're only charged when customers click on your ad
- Minimum total campaign budget of $100
- Choose a custom date range

Understand Your Campaign Dashboard

Once you have one or more ads created, you will see them on your campaign dashboard in a table. On top, you will find the button to create new campaigns with a search field next to it. On the right side, you see a button with an icon, which points to a hard drive. Here you can download your campaigns in CSV format. Right next to it you can select the results - how many campaigns you want to see per page. The default value is 25.

What is a CSV File?

In computing, a comma-separated values (CSV) file is a delimited text file that uses a comma to separate values. A CSV file stores tabular data (numbers and text) in plain text. Each line of the file is a data record. Each record consists of one or more fields, separated by commas. The use of the comma as a field separator is the source of the name for this file format.

The Search Option

If you have more than 25 campaigns they won't fit any longer one page. You can switch to 50 or 100 view, however, next time you update or refresh the page it goes back to the 25 rows per page view.

This feature is also helpful because it works in real-time. For example, if you only want to see campaigns that contain the word ‚money‘ write this into the search field. I use it mostly to sort my campaigns by status. After a few months you may have several active campaigns, also paused campaigns and maybe campaigns that you terminated. So, if you put ‚run‘ into the search field you only get running campaigns in your overview.

Metrics Are Delayed up to 14 Days

Above your summary table, you see the following sentence: „Campaign metrics may take up to 14 days to appear and do not include Kindle Unlimited or Kindle Owner Lending Library royalties generated by the ad.“

From my experience, 14 days delay never happened, but it's hard to track. Usually, I see my sales after a few days reported. How do I know? Because you also have your Kindle direct publishing reports where you look at your daily sales. You know from this statistic which books and how many you sold per day.

Campaign Columns Explained

The first column list the status of your campaigns. Once your ads are approved, you will see a green button labeled ‚Running‘. Clicking on this button gives you the option to pause or terminate the ad. Other status options are ‚Ended‘ or ‚Rejected‘. Sponsored product ads have the option to set the duration with an open-end - meaning they run as long as you either pause or terminate them. Product display ads have a length of maximum six months.

The Campaign Name

That's the name of your ad, and you should pay attention to how you create that name. Nothing more confusing than the same name with just the number on end, which is basically what the Amazon system does. When we come to creating ads, I will explain this in more details and also give you tips on how you effectively name your ads.

Start & End Date

That's pretty obvious as it shows the start and the end date of each campaign. Again, please know that Product display ads run a maximum of six months, where Sponsored product ads have the option for an open-end duration. If you see in End Date just a dash, that means its length is open.

Budget

Depending on the what ad version you are running this either shows you the daily limit or the limit for the complete duration of the campaign. Don't be hesitant to put a high number in there - it does not mean you have to pay all of it.

The Sponsored product ads have a daily limit. I have set them in my campaign mostly to $10, in some cases, where I thought I get more exposure, to $20. Never since I started with ads has one of my campaigns reached that limit!

The Product display ads have their budget set to the whole duration of the ad campaign - a maximum of 6 months. I usually put $200 in there, sometimes even up to $500. Again, don't be shocked by the amount, you only pay for clicks that actually happened.

It's better you put in a higher than a lower amount. If you go to low your ad may run out of steam without you noticing it. When you finally notice it, you have to increase your budget, and it may take a few days until your ad is fully distributed again.

Please note that all further columns show accumulated data.

This means that you don't get a daily statistic on your ad performance. All data is accumulated over time. This is a considerable disadvantage, and when you ever advertised with Google, you may get the impression that the Amazon stats are technical way behind. However, we will come to that problem a bit later, and I will show you a few ideas on how to overcome that problem. For now, that's all you need to know.

Impressions

Amazon states that an impression is generated every time your ad is displayed. An impression (in the context of online advertising) is when an ad is fetched from its source and is countable. Whether the ad is clicked is not taken into account. Each time an ad is fetched, it is counted as one impression.

Counting impressions is the method by which most web advertising is accounted and paid for, and the cost is quoted in CPI (cost per impression). In contrast to CPC, which is the cost per click and not impression-based.

Amazon uses the pay per click model and not the cost per impression model.

That's an important fact because it means that every time your ad shows a visitor could discover your book without you paying for it.

Why is this an advantage?

Let's say a reader sees your ad a view times but does not click on the ad. A few days later the reader somehow recalls your book ad - maybe triggered by looking at something similar. Wanting to get more information the reader remembers the title or your name and starts a search in Google. If you are lucky the reader either finds your homepage or the Amazon link to your book. Now, with a bit more luck, the reader clicks on one of the links and ends up buying your book.

You just sold a book with zero advertising cost!

The story I made up above may not reflect the usual consumer behavior, however there so many other ways how your ad exposure could eventually trigger a book sale.

If you do not pay for impressions, every time your ad appears without being clicked, your book gets free exposure. This is very powerful and can lead to many sales without you paying not even a penny.

Clicks

Clicks are where the magic happens. A click is generated when a user clicks or taps your ad. Amazon then redirects the reader to your designated book page, where the buy button is just one more click away.

It's important to remember, that before clicks it was tough to track ads. The effectiveness of ads was based on guesses or excessively complicated (but ultimately untestable) maths. Advertisers would put up a billboard poster, buy some radio or TV time and run your spot and then wait. If your profits went up, you would assume your advertising worked, but you wouldn't know for sure. With the measurable nature of clicks (and conversions), now you can know for sure whether ads are driving readers to your book description page.

There is also a considerable discrepancy from country to country. According to Google Display Benchmarks, New Zealand has a CTR of around 0.87% whereas the UK and US hover about 0.1%, meaning Kiwis click on ads almost nine times as often as Brits or Americans. And it's not just because that's the trend down under - Australians CTR hovers around 0.2%.

For clicks, you must pay, and the amount depends on how much your bid is, as well as how many other advertisers use the same keyword or targeted book.

The Average Cost per Click (aCPC)

This number shows your total campaign spend divided by the total number of clicks the campaign generated. For example, if your 'ad spend' is $10 and the amount of clicks you generated with your ad is 100, than the average cost per click is 10 cent. It's an average because the price per clicks varies over time. This is because the amount of other advertisers bidding for the same keyword or book never stays the same.

What you pay per click depends on how many other advertisers bid for the same keyword or target the same book with their ad. Bids could be as low as 5 cents and as high as 50 cents. I have not seen anything higher than 46 cents in my own campaigns. However, there may be categories that have much higher CPC's due to high demand on customers for that particular book genre.

When your keyword is broad it is highly likely you pay more if it is very specific and contains more than 2-3 words it's likely very cheap.

Spend

This column shows you the amount you have spent so far on a particular ad campaign. There is not much further to say that this column gets essential for calculating your ROI (Return on Investment).

Estimated Total Sales

Here is how Amazon defines that column: This shows you the total price of orders customers placed after clicking your ad. This may include the removal of purchases that were canceled within 72 hours of the initial purchase or any declined purchases. Your KDP sales reports will show you the final sales numbers, which may be different from the number you see here.

You would think that this is the most important column - it's not! We come to the last column ACoS in a minute, which is the most important number you want to watch.

The sales amount you will see is the amount your reader pays for your book. That may be different than the amount you have set in your KDP bookshelf. Amazon may discount your book without you noticing. However, rest assured that this will not cut into your earnings - it will exactly stay the same as you can see it in your KDP bookshelf.

So, if you see the sales price of your Kindle book at $7.95, then this amount will show up in this column when you made a sale. This is important to remember when we later want to calculate your return on investment (ROI) - with other words how much money you made (hopefully) on one book sale.

Advertising Cost of Sales (ACoS)

Advertising Cost of Sales is the amount you've spent on a campaign divided by total sales during the campaign run dates. In general, a lower ACoS is more desirable than a higher ACoS. That means you're spending fewer dollars to generate the same amount of revenue.

ACoS is one of the most critical measurements when it comes to determining if your ads are successful. I have an extra chapter, where I can explain this in detail.

The Action Button

Last, but not least we have that action column, which currently only offers you the option to make a copy for your current ad. There is just one important thing to know here. Immediately after you create a copy of your current ad, please change the name of your ad. Amazon only adds a (1) behind the current name, which may keep you guessing later what this ad campaign is all about.

Once you submitted your new ad, you can't change the name anymore. When you have several ads, you want to separate them by a meaningful name!

What we covered so far was your advertising campaigns dashboard menu. The next few paragraphs are about billing history and the payment setting menus. I will only go over it briefly, and once you have this setup, you won't need it as much as the main dashboard.

The Billing History Menu

This shows your current invoice and also all past statements. In the beginning, there may be shorter periods of invoices for maybe $20 or $50. Later on, once you have past one month, Amazon will make one statement per month. At least that's what my billing history table shows. Let me know if you see other forms of payment statements on your dashboard.

Here is what I found on the official help page:

Amazons billing occurs periodically depending on the total charges accumulated. You may be billed more frequently at the start of a campaign, but you will never be billed more than the actual cost of clicks. Amazons billing system is set up to only charge your credit card as the campaign receives clicks.

Amazon don't charges your card for the entire campaign budget upfront because they cannot guarantee that they will deliver the entire budget. Amazon also wants to give you the opportunity to pause your campaign at any time and still only pay for the clicks you actually received.

If you pay with your credit card, you are not provided with notifications of billing. You are billed for your ads when:

- Your account accumulates your first $1.00 worth of clicks.

- Your account accumulates additional clicks that meet or exceed your credit limit. Your credit limit begins at $50 and increases each time you reach your credit limit and you make a successful payment. From $50 it increases to $150, $200, $350, and finally $500.

- You have a balance due for the previous month, regardless of your credit limit. You incur this charge on the third day of each month.

Payment Settings Option

Currently there only payment option is by debit or credit card. You can set up more than one credit card, for example, a primary card and a backup card. I suggest that you have an eye on your billing and funds on your card.

If a payment is declined because of insufficient funds all your ads are stopped! You can add another card or initiate a new payment transaction after you have enough funds on your card. However, it can take 1-2 days - even more if it is a weekend - where your ads are not shown.

Submit a second credit card information as a backup option in case your primary card is declined or runs out of funds.

Chapter 3 - Setting the Path to Success

What Royalty Plan Should I Choose?

Most of the following section refer to the Kindle ebook. There is an extra chapter where I inform you about the pricing option for the Paperback, Hardcover, and audiobook version. The easiest option is to start with an ebook, which you can set up in less than 20 minutes.

Benefits of the 70% Royalty Plan

Your first choice probably goes to the 70% royalty plan. Let us break down the advantages and disadvantages of this price option.

You need to price your ebook between $2.99 and $9.99, and you will pay an additional fee for file delivery. The price for delivery to U.S. buyers is $0.15 per megabyte. (e.g. subtract $0.75 from your royalty if your ebook size is 5 MB.) This means you have to pay attention to using images in your ebook.

Images could get very large in file size if you don't know how to compress them.

I once uploaded one of my financial dictionaries and forgot to crunch the cover image. Only a few months later I discovered how big that file was and that I paid over $3 in delivery cost. It left me with just $2.50 instead of $5.00 - a huge difference and what a waste of money. By the way, Amazon is the only ebook distributor who charges you with delivery fees. I think that this business model is outdated, but that's another story. Let's focus on making the best of what we got.

I have some image optimization tools that I recommend which you will find in the resource section.

You get 70% in most major territories, in all others you get 35%. The territories where you get 70% are the U.S. and most of Europe.

Your book must be part of KDP Select if you want the 70% royalty on ebook sales in Brazil, India, Japan or Mexico. You also agree to allow buyers to lend their copy of your book. This is only a one-time, 14-day loan each ebook license holder can make after buying your book. Nothing to worry here.

What is KDP Select?

Enrolling your ebook in Amazons optional KDP Select program gives you the opportunity to reach more readers and earn more money. You can enroll a single book, your whole catalog or anything in between. Enrolling in KDP Select makes your book eligible for 70% royalty earnings on sales to customers in Brazil, Japan, India, and Mexico.

If you make your eBook exclusive to the Kindle Store, which is a requirement during your book's enrollment in KDP Select, the book will also be included in Kindle Unlimited (KU) and the Kindle Owners' Lending Library (KOLL). You can earn a share of the KDP Select Global Fund based on how many pages KU or KOLL customers read of your book.

This can affect your book earnings dramatically. If you have a novel with 500 pages and people are engaged in your novel, and it read it all the way to the end you get paid $0.005 * 500 = $2.50. If you sell 100 books per month than that's an extra $250 income!

Enrolling in KDP Select also grants you access to a new set of promotional tools. You can schedule a Kindle Countdown Deal (limited time promotional discounting for your book) for books available on Amazon.com and Amazon.co.uk or a Free Book Promotion (readers worldwide can get your book free for a limited time).

This feature is also great, and I will get into book marketing with this feature later on in this book.

You Must Give Amazon Exclusivity

When you enroll an ebook in KDP Select, you're committing to making the digital format of that book available exclusively through KDP while it's enrolled in the program. You can continue to distribute your book in physical format or in any format other than digital.

All content enrolled in KDP Select must remain for sale through the Kindle Store only. If the digital version of your book appears to be available for pre-order, for sale, or for free elsewhere (such as on your website or blog, or a third party's website), it is not eligible for KDP Select.

Adding new content (such as bonus content, author's commentary section, etc.) to a book that's available elsewhere will not satisfy the exclusivity requirements. See the KDP Select terms and conditions for complete exclusivity requirements.

You can opt-out of KDP Select after a 90 days period. If you fail to opt-out a few days before that period you automatically get enrolled in another 90 days period.

Benefits of the 35% Royalty Plan

The only advantage I can see is if you publish ebooks with many and large images, as Amazon will not charge you on delivery fees with this plan.

You may also choose to sell your book above the $10 limit for the 70% royalty option. This may also be a better choice if you publish material for a narrow niche market or an exclusive market. For example, you sell exclusive statistics for market research.

It also makes sense to choose that option if you already have clients that are eager to purchase your book and you don't depend on any advertising or marketing cost.

New 50% Royalty Plan in Beta

Amazon is currently (2018) testing a 50% Kindle royalties option for nonfiction books that meet specific eligibility standards. Great on Kindle is an Amazon program to help customers discover high-quality nonfiction eBooks. Great on Kindle eBooks offer enhanced features that readers value.

This program is currently an invite-only beta and on a book-by-book basis.

What Are Your Benefits?

If your nonfiction eBook qualifies for Great on Kindle, it will be eligible for:

- A detail page message that identifies it as a high-quality book
- Promotional credit offers for customers (this won't affect your royalty)
- Nominations for potential merchandising opportunities
- A 50% royalty plan if the book's list price meets requirements

The new, optional, 50% royalty makes it more lucrative for selling nonfiction books if publishers meet specific criteria. Great on Kindle also introduces a new pricing tier requiring participating nonfiction books to be priced between $4.99 and $19.99 to receive the 50% royalty. This new plan and does not deduct delivery costs from your royalty.

What Are the Requirements?

To qualify for Great on Kindle, your nonfiction eBook must be available for sale on amazon.com and meet the program's quality standards.

1. Make sure all images are high resolution
2. Make sure Enhanced Typesetting is enabled
3. Enter unique, accurate book details
4. Enable X-Ray
5. Correct any typos or formatting errors
6. Set up an Author Page

I don't have more information at this time but will inform you (sign up link and additional information at the end of the book) when this program is available for the public or how you can participate in the Beta.

Please find the complete details (all country options) and requirements for each royalty plan in the Amazon KDP help section. I have included that link in the resource page at the end of this book.

Paperback Royalty Plan

Amazon offers a fixed 60% royalty rate on paperbacks sold on Amazon marketplaces where KDP supports paperback distribution. Your royalty is 60% of your list price. They subtract printing costs, which depend on page count, ink type, and the Amazon marketplace your paperback was ordered from.

(Royalty rate x list price) – printing costs = royalty

For example, your list price is $15. Your book is a 333-page paperback with black ink sold on the US marketplace:

Your royalty calculation is: (0.60 x $15) - $4.85 = **$4.15**

If you enable ‚Expanded Distribution', the royalty is 40% of the book's list price effective in the distribution channel at the time of purchase minus printing costs.

(Royalty rate x list price) – printing costs = royalty

For example, your list price is $15. Your book is a 333-page paperback with black ink sold through Expanded Distribution channels:

Your royalty calculation is:(0.40 x $15) - $4.85 = **$1.15**

What's The Best Price Point for my Book?

Let's start of with some recent market studies...

During the survey for the United States in 2017 [11], 16 percent of respondents stated that they were willing to pay between two and 3.99 U.S. dollars for an e-book if the price of the corresponding paperback was 14 U.S. dollars. During the same survey, 20 percent of female respondents stated that they were willing to pay between four and 5.99 U.S. dollars for an e-book if the price of the corresponding paperback was 14 U.S. dollars.

Also 21 percent of respondents aged 60 and older stated that they were willing to pay between two and 3.99 U.S. dollars for an e-book if the price of the corresponding paperback was 14 U.S. dollars. During the same survey, 56 percent of respondents stated that they completely agreed with the statement that e-books should be cheaper than the printed version.

According to Statista's analysts, you would sell more ebooks if you use a price structure that passes on the cost advantage that ebooks have over printed books to the readers. Looking at current bestsellers in the United States reveals that the ebook editions of the Top 10 bestsellers in the U.S. are roughly 20 percent cheaper than the corresponding hardcover editions.

A few years ago Amazon gave the public a peek into its data around prices and e-book sales. The Amazon Books Team posted on the following on the Kindle Forum:

For every copy an e-book would sell at $14.99, it would sell 1.74 copies if priced at $9.99. So, for example, if customers would buy 100,000 copies of a particular e-book at

$14.99, then customers would buy 174,000 copies of that same e-book at $9.99. Total revenue at $14.99 would be $1,499,000. Total revenue at $9.99 is $1,738,000.

Shoppers Price Psychology

In the general psychology of shopping (not just in the world of books), people lean to associate price with quality. If product A costs twice as much as similar product B, then product B must be a lower quality than the expensive brand. There may be zero evidence to support this conclusion, but some people still believe it.

For this reason, you're not doing yourself any favors by selling your 400-page novel for only 99 cents. The low price could lead readers to conclude that there must be something wrong with the quality of the book.

On the other hand, having a 99 cent sale for a limited time is an entirely different story. When you let the reader know that your average sales price is $7.95 and you have a 48 hours 99 cents sale, then this sends a different message to your reader. They understand that you have a great book and you have it on sale.

Reasons to Price Your Book at 99 Cents

A 99 cents price point is a no-brainer, and an impulse-priced book allows a reader to take a chance on a book that looks interesting. If you're an unknown author trying to build your readership base, this might be the answer.[12]

To rise to the top of Amazon rankings is the goal for any author. Amazon counts book sales units, not revenue. Setting your price at the impulse level of $0.99 could help you glide up in the ranking and gain visibility there. With that visibility, other people in the publishing field may take notice.

When you visit your book page, you'll see a section that says "Customers Who Bought This Item Also Bought." The real value for you is when your book appears in that section on other successful books. Amazon will list up to 100 books in this section and readers will often scroll through that list to discover other books that look interesting. A drop to a 99 cents sales price may be the incentive to increase your sales to place your book in a popular section with more exposure.

In the last few years indie authors engaged in a price war to sell their books and find new readers. Where before you had not seen many books priced at 99 cents, there are now thousands of books available for that price. I only recommend selling your book for 99 cents if it has a low page count of mate 10.000 words. Besides that, you can use a 99 cents price if you do a book launch, or have it a few days on sale.

Many websites promote your book for free or with a fee if it is priced for 99 cents. You will find a list of them in the resource section on the end of this book.

Best Price Range for Maximum Revenue

You'll find countless authors who are enjoying success at the currently popular price levels of $4.99 to $9.99. To encourage more readers with a low price and still get the 70% royalty, you would set your price to $2.99.

However, writing and publishing an ebook is more than just numbers, dollars, and cents. These kinds of royalty calculations are only one factor in the success of your book.

According to WrittenWord[13] the price that maximizes author royalties is the same this year as it was last year, $3.99. Readers are more discerning at higher price points and are unwilling to spend $3.99 on titles with poor book covers or no or few reviews.

They were looking at sales that came through Amazon, and on Amazon, authors receive 70% of every sale they make when their book is priced between $2.99 and $9.99, and 35% of the sale when their book is priced below $2.99. This means that you need to sell much more copies at $0.99 or $1.99 than you do at a higher price point in order to make the same amount of money.

KDP Select Affects Your Earnings

Authors enrolled in KDP Select are more likely to be able to achieve high sales numbers and high earnings when they choose to run price promotions. The reason for this are these two factors:

- Kindle Countdown Deals
- KENP Payouts.

Based on tests performed by WrittenWords[14], authors on average see a 1300 bump in KENP reads the day of the promotion, with reads increasing into the weeks after the promotion. With the current payout per page amount averaging $0.0045, that's an additional $5.85 in earnings per day that an author earns off the promotion.

Here are a few more interesting results from their market survey:

Psychological thrillers are still all the rage. Many of the best performing books at higher price points ($3.99 and $4.99) were psychological thrillers. Reviews and backlist help readers make purchasing decisions. Also on the lower end of the sales spectrum were the books with few to no reviews.

Presumed Price Points From a Buyer Perspective

A price between $0 - $0.99 is a no-brainer if I am interested I may give it a try without even looking further into ratings and book description.

A sales price between $0.99 - $2.99 sounds reasonable, and the price will not engage me into hitting the buy button right away. I may look closer at reviews and book description. I may put it on my wishlist of interesting books.

A sales price between $2.99 - $5.99 reflects a good value, but it's not a bargain. Is this a well-known author? Any other books that the author has written?

A sales price between $5.99 - $9.99 may seem on the upper end, even if this is from one of the five big publishers. If this is fiction, it better be on the New York Times top 10 sales list. If it is non-fiction, I may take a closer look. My interest may switch over to the Paperback edition.

If your sales price is above $10.00, it's probably for a niche market. I really need it for work or my business. I may buy it because I am in a hurry to read it and I don't want to wait until it arrives in the mail.

Look at Similar Books

You could also look at other books that are similar to yours and collect some details about them. Start by looking at the category on Amazon where you think your book fits. Then write down the following:

- Kindle selling price
- Paperback selling price
- List price for the paperback (discounted price)
- Page count
- Number of reviews
- Rating from reviews

In the resource section you will find a link to FixMyStory[15], where Jordan Smith provides a spreadsheet template to fill in with all of those details.

Make Your Book Free

Why would you do that? There are several good reasons for making your book permanently free. Yes, you can price your book for free on Amazon. However, the only way I know of right now is contacting them and requesting to set the price to zero.

One reason to do this is lead generation. You or your business may offer something else than books. Maybe you have a video course, or you sell a web service. Creating a book or booklet about a specific topic could send interested people to you. Of course, that only works if your free book is somehow popular on Amazon and you have included an additional offer in your book. For example, a discount code that's not available anywhere else.

I have my financial terms dictionary ,100 Most Popular Financial Terms Explained' permanently free on Amazon, and it refers to my other 12 books on that series. It supports selling them very well.

Creating it was easy by merely extracting the content from my other books. The most work was going into research and deciding what the 100 most important financial terms may be. Once in a while, someone orders the Paperback version for $12.95! The Kindle ranking is most of the time between 10.000 and 20.000.

Another reason to make a book free is author exposure. If you have several other books on Amazon, you could use a freebie to spark interest in your other books. You send them to your website and let them sign up with their email address to get the latest author information and maybe an expert from your next upcoming book.

However, even you may use your book as a lead generation you may still sell it for $0.99 or even higher. It all depends on which niche market you operate and how high the demand for the information is that you provide.

Use the KDP Pricing Tool

You can also use Amazon's Kindle pricing tool to get price suggestions. Go to the KDP Edit Rights, Royalty and Pricing section of your book's details and click the big View Service button under the Pricing Support header. This will show a tool that examines books similar to yours on the Kindle store, then suggests a price that can maximize your earnings.

It also tells you what price might maximize the number of sales you'll get. This tool won't tell you how many books you may sell, but check it out and consider it when you set the price of your book. The recommendation of this tool changes over time as the Kindle store data changes. You may check it once in a while to see any shift in the market.

What is the Story with Impressions?

Impressions are the number that reflects how many times your ad has been shown on Amazon. Again, it's important to understand that every impression is an attempt to catch the interest of a potential buyer. If the ad is at a place where the eye of a visitor glances it's highly likely the visitor sees your ad. Of course, it doesn't mean the visitor clicks on it; however, it went into the sub-conscious.

A lot has been written about the psychology of advertising. At this point, just understand that every impression your ad generates makes some waves and you don't pay anything for it. After a person has seen your ad several times and is, at later point presented with a selection of books, that person will recognize your book and at that point may make a buying decision.

Your ad should generate as many impressions as possible. The more impressions your ad gets, the more clicks it could produce, and therefore the more sales you can have. So far the theory.

Sponsored Product Ads

If you use this keyword-based advertising method, you can expect to generate about one click per thousand impressions. This measurement is also called Click Through Rate or CTR. It's the number of impressions decided by the number of clicks. e.g:

1000 impressions / 1 click = 0.1%

That's a basic number calculated from many ads and also taking into account experiences from other advertisers. Yours may be better or worse.

Product Display Ads

This ad type generates more clicks with less impressions. In an average your Click Trough Rate (CTR) maybe in the range of 0.6%-1.0%.

If you get not enough impressions for your ad you need to look at these facts:

- Do you have enough keywords in your ad campaign?
- Do you have keywords that people are typing into the search box of Amazon?
- Have you tried increasing your bid price?
- Is your targeted category to narrow?
- Have you tried different categories?

Does My Ad Get Enough Clicks?

After your ad gets viewed a few hundred or thousand times someone finally may click on it and gets to your book's landing page. For this click, you have to pay. The amount depends on how many other advertisers are bidding on the same keyword or the same category. You will see this number in your Amazon advertising dashboard under the column aCPC (average cost per click).

Overall CTR Benchmark

The best source for display CTR benchmarks was originally DoubleClick (the display advertising part of Google) who have this regularly updated interactive Display Benchmarking tool as part of Think Insights. Google merged DoubleClick into their own Google Adwords a while ago, and rebranded it as Google Ads. Unfortunately, the latest figures are for April 2017 [16].

Across all ad formats and placements display ad CTR is just 0.05%

I could not get a statistic on average click-through rates from KDP advertising. From my experience, it seems it is in the range of 0.1%. The reason for that, I believe, is the mindset of an Amazon visitor. Amazon is primarily a shopping site and offers a search engine on top of that. Visitors on Amazon are looking to buy a product and are ready to pull out their credit card when they find the right product. They may even don't need their credit card if they have set up the ‚One Click' buy option.

The One-Click has become even more important as online shopping on mobile devices becomes more common. Because mobile screens are small, the larger the hassle or number of clicks it is to purchase, the lower the purchase propensity on mobile phones.

On Google that's a different story, because the majority of people look for information.

So, if your ad gets enough impressions, you should see a fair amount of clicks from it. If your ad reaches a high amount of impressions and only a few clicks then you have to look at the following issues:

- Is your ad targeting the right audience?
- Is your ad text compelling and makes people click?
- Does your book has a professional cover?
- Is your book title interesting to Readers?
- Is your price too high?

Check these facts and start either updating your campaign, adding an ad variation or launch an entirely new ad. Experimenting and patience is the key here to success. Advertising on Amazon is not a set and forget approach. Let me know of an honest business where this is possible.

Please note, that when your ad has a very low click-through rate over a longer period, Amazon may terminate it due to bad performance. Most likely your ad targets the wrong audience.

Amazon and other platforms like Google are interested that the ads are relevant to the visitors. If they aren't, a visitor or potential buyer gets too much distracted, and they abandon the site. Google won the search competition by showing more relevant searches to their users. They changed their algorithm years ago already from a ‚keyword' based search to a ‚meaning' search. They even hired one of the smartest guys - Ray Kurzweil - to build a search engine that works like a brain. You will find some book recommendation in the resource section.

Amazon probably won the e-commerce shopping race because they streamlined their shopping experience with a one-click checkout, never had a security breach, and also provides the best search engine for a shopping site.

What is a Conversion?

A conversion is a book sale that originated from an ad.

After impressions and clicks follow sales - at least this should happen. It's a long way from the first impression to a book sale. Your ad should target the right audience, and it should be compelling and lead to people clicking on it. After they land on your designated book page, they need to find what they expected from your ad!

If you go exaggerate too much with your ad text, and you promise too much of what you can't deliver on your book landing page, your potential buyer is turned off, and you missed out on the sale.

It's better your book landing page continues with what your book title and ad text say. This way, you keep your potential buyer in the funnel until they hit the buy button. On your dedicated book page you should have a professional book cover and a compelling book description. We will later cover this topic in an extra chapter.

A conversion is a success, but it does not automatically mean you made money! If you have made your first sale from an ad, please get into the happy mood and give yourself some kudos. You have done a great job by creating an ad that has sold one or more of your books.

What is ROI & ACoS?

ROI is the short form of return on investment. It's basically how much money you make, and it can be calculated in dollar or percentage. Return on investment represents the financial benefit received from an investment.

It's a measure of what you get back compared to what you put in. It's used in many areas of finance, as well as in business. In business, it's most often used to determine the effectiveness of marking, although that's not the only area you can measure ROI.[17]

When it comes to ROI, your goal is to have maximum return for minimal investment. You want to get more back than what you put in.

Why ROI Is Important?

Calculating ROI can help you understand what's working and not working in your business so you can make changes. If your book ad isn't generating a profit, then you're losing money. Knowing that would then prompt you to either change the ad to improve ROI or ditch it all together.

Amazon ROI is ACoS

Amazon uses the term ACoS, and it means your advertising cost of sales, It is the amount you've spent on a campaign divided by total sales during the campaign run dates.

Here's an example:

If your ad campaign has generated $300 in sales with an expenditure of $75 over a certain period, then the ACoS = 75 / 300 = 0.25, in percentage 25%. In other words, you're spending a quarter on ads to make one dollar of sales with that ad campaign. Now, that number doesn't tell you much. You want to find your actual return on investment.

Many advertisers use ACoS to determine the success of their ad campaigns. The difficulty in this, however, is defining the right target value for an ACoS – because the ACoS alone doesn't say anything about how profitable a campaign is. To determine whether a certain ACoS is good or bad, you'll need to take the entire cost structure of your book into account.

The sales price is higher than what you earn. That's why using the ACoS from Amazon is somehow misleading. You need to find out the break-even point of ACoS.

How to Determine your Break Even ACoS

As a book author, you won't incur a loss on sponsored product campaigns as long as you spend less than your profit margin on the advertisement. The profit margin is the amount you make after all costs and fees are subtracted from the selling price.

When you sell a Kindle book than you are either on a 35% or 70% royalty plan. Let's look at each royalty plan in detail.

Royalty Calculations

If you select the 35% royalty option, your royalty will be 35% of your list price without VAT (taxes) for each unit sold.

If you select the 70% royalty option, your royalty will be 70% of your list price without VAT, less delivery costs (average delivery costs are $0.06 per unit sold, and vary by file size), for each eligible book sold to customers in the 70% territories, and 35% of the list price for each unit sold to customers residing outside the 70% territories.

If Amazon sells your digital book at a price below your list price without VAT in order to match price with a third party selling any digital or physical edition of the book, or to match Amazon's price for a physical edition of the book, you will receive 70% of our sale price for each eligible book sold to customers in the 70% territories, less delivery costs, and less any applicable VAT.

Kindle Books Delivery Costs

Amazon charges delivery costs if you are on the 70% royalty plan. No charges apply on the 35% royalty plan. Delivery Costs are equal to the number of megabytes Amazon determines your Digital Book file contain, multiplied by the Delivery Cost rate listed below.

- Amazon.com: US $0.15/MB
- Amazon.ca: CAD $0.15/MB
- Amazon.com.br: R$0.30/MB
- Amazon.co.uk: UK £0.10/MB
- Amazon.de: €0,12/MB
- Amazon.fr: €0,12/MB
- Amazon.es: €0,12/MB
- Amazon.it: €0,12/MB
- Amazon.nl: €0,12/MB
- Amazon.co.jp: ¥1/MB
- Amazon.com.mx: MXN $1/MB
- Amazon.com.au: AUD $0.15/MB

Amazon will round file sizes up to the nearest kilobyte. The minimum Delivery Cost for a Digital Book will be US$0.01 for sales in US Dollars, CAD$0.01 for sales in CAD Dollars, £0.01 for sales in GB Pounds, ¥1 in JPY, R$0.01 for sales in Brazilian Reais, MXN$1 for sales in Mexican Pesos, AUD$0.01 for sales in Australian Dollars, and €0.01 for sales in Euros, regardless of file size. For sales in JPY, we will not deduct any Delivery Cost for books 10 MB or higher.

Final ROI Calculation Example

So, as we now have all the cost and the royalty plan, we can calculate the real ROI. Let's assume you sales price of your Kindle book is $10, and you are on a 70% royalty plan. Let's further assume that your Kindle book is 3MB in size. You can see the file size on your dedicated book page under the topic Product Details.

When we take 70% from $10, we have $7. From that amount, we deduct the delivery cost of $0.15 x 3MB = $0.45. Your profit on that book would then be $7 - $0.45 = $6.55. In our case, that's 65.5% of the sales price.

With that number, we can now calculate your break-even ACoS. Remember, ACoS was the amount you spend on a particular campaign divided by the number of sales. Let's go back to our example with the $300 in sales.

We now divide that number by 100 and then multiply it by 65.5%. This comes out to $196.50. As the last step we take our $75 spend amount and divide it by $196.50. The result is our ACoS with 38.2%. That's a different number than the 25% we had before!

Now, what interest us is the ACoS break-even point. Anything below that number is profit, and everything above that number is a loss.

How Do Calculate the Break Even ACoS?

Let's use the sales price of $10 for our book again. We have determined that we earn $6.55 on this book (70% revenue share + delivery costs subtracted). If we would spend $10 and sell one book for $10, Amazon would show you an ACoS number of 100%. However, we already know that we can't use that number.

We already have that number figured out before. We have established that for $1 we spend we could make a maximum profit of $0.655. If we relate that number to 100%, then we get 65.5%, and that's our break-even ACoS.

With other words, your break-even ACoS in percentage is your royalty payment minus any additional costs (delivery fees) divided by your sales price multiplied by 100. Let's look at our example again:

ACoS Break Even Example with 70% Royalty Plan

Sales price:	$10
Royalty 70%:	$7
Delivery costs:	$0.45 (3MB)
Profit:	$6.55 ($7-$0.45)
ACoS Break Even:	0.655 ($6.55 / $10)
ACoS Break Even %:	65.5% (0.655 * 100)

If you are doing lower than 65.5%, we'll be profitable. If we are doing over 65.5%, you will be unprofitable.

ACoS Break Even Example with 35% Royalty Plan

Sales price: $10

Royalty 70%: $3.50

Delivery costs: $0

Profit: $3.50 ($3.50-$0)

ACoS Break Even: 0.35 ($3.50 / $10)

ACoS Break Even %:   35% (0.35 * 100)

If you are doing lower than 35%, we'll be profitable. If you are doing over 35%, we will be unprofitable.

Chapter 4 - Make Your Book Discoverable with Keywords

The Importance of Using the Right Keywords

Keywords are the lifeline for your Sponsored products ads. Finding and using the right keywords for your ad campaign is essential. If your keywords do not relate to your book, you are wasting your ad money, and your ACoS will be too high to earn money from your book sales.

There are many things that you can do wrong with your keyword selection. Most of the mistakes I have seen fall into one of these categories.

Common Mistakes of Using Keywords

- Using only the Google keyword suggestion tool
- Using keywords nobody is searches in Amazon
- Going too broad with a single keyword
- Going too narrow with a long tail keyword phrase
- Using high competitive keywords
- Using keywords that don't match your book content

First Steps on Choosing Keywords

Combine keywords in the most logical order. Customers search for "military science fiction" but probably not for "fiction science military". Before publishing, search for your book's title and keywords on Amazon. If you get irrelevant or unsatisfying results, make some changes. When searching, look at the suggestions that appear in the "Search" field drop-down box.

Think like a reader. Imagine how you'd search if you were a customer.

Not Allowed Keywords

Amazon program names like as ‚Kindle Unlimited' or ‚KDP Select' are not allowed to use.

How Do I Find Relevant Keywords?

Use Amazons' Search Suggestion

This is a very powerful way to find related keywords. We will use Amazons' keyword suggestion tool. For this to work in your favour, please log out of your account. As a second step, please use the incognito or private mode in your browser.

- Chrome - Open new incognito mode tab or window
- Firefox - Open new private tab or window
- Safari - Open new private tab or window

If you use another browser, the functionality may be different. We are doing this because the Amazon suggestion feature uses your accounts information as well as browser cookies to match the results. In incognito or private mode, you'll get raw data – which is what we want.

Now go to Amazon, select the Kindle category from the department selection, and use one of your primary keywords. Something you may find in the description of your book or a simple phrase that describes your book genre (e.g. science fiction thriller, financial investment). When you put in ‚science fiction' Amazon shows you a few other suggestions that people already used. In our example you may see:

- science fiction romance
- science fiction and fantasy
- science fiction space war
- science fiction anthology
- science fiction short stories

You can do this with any major keyword and find related keywords people are using to find and buy books.

We can go even further with this tool and add one letter from the alphabet at the end of our phrase ‚science fiction'. This will then look like this ‚science fiction a'. Now Amazon gives you all keywords people have already used that start with the letter ‚a'. In this case, you may see this:

- science fiction aliens
- science fiction adventure
- science fiction and philosophy

You know already what comes next? You take the next letter from the alphabet and do the same until you get to the end of the alphabet. Yes, that's very time-consuming. However, it ensures you are only targeting keywords that people are looking for.

Finding good keywords is a complex task, and many people wondered if we can't use power tools to expedite that process. Indeed, there are meanwhile a dozen or more services and programs that offer help with that task. I tried many of them - if not all - and most of them are not useful. They either don't suggest relevant keywords, or they are missing essential information about how often they are used.

What good will a keyword be for you if users are only searching for it five times per month? In our first attempt by using Amazons' own search suggestion we get relevant keywords, but we don't know the monthly volume.

Find Related Keywords

If your book has been on Amazon for a time, look at your book's detail page. If it's only just been put up, find a book similar to yours and make a note of the books suggested underneath.

If they seem even remotely similar to yours (The 'Customers who viewed this item also viewed' section and the 'Sponsored products related to this item' section). Add the title and author name of each of them to your keyword list.

List all the books you can think of, that are similar to your book. Add the title and author name of each of them to your keyword list.

There are many other ways to get your keyword list established. However, most of these additional methods are very time-consuming. I want you to use only the best, and most efficient ways, and not waste your valuable time with complex and challenging approaches.

Some of the tools I recommend are pricey, others are very reasonable, and I even have some great free tools that work very well.

So, let's move on to the more advanced tools and services that can provide you with plenty of relevant keywords. The first tool I am suggesting is also one of the best - it is KDP Rocket.

Find Keywords with KDP Rocket

KDP Rocket will find keywords that readers are actually typing into Amazon, and that puts this tool already at the top of the list. As I mentioned there are plenty of other tools, however, most of them are not using keywords that people typed into Amazon.

Dave Chesson developed it. He published a few successful books, but soon expanded into helping other authors with his blog ‚Kindlepreneur'. He also published a free course on advertising, which I recommend and you find on his website. More details in the resource section of this book.

Let's get into the rocket...

Unlike any other software, KDP Rocket gives you real data that shows you exactly what Amazon book buyers type into Amazon, as well as how many people search for these things every month. Here are the main facts:

- What keywords shoppers type into Amazon
- Estimated number of times someone types that keyword into Amazon
- How much money other books are making that rank for that keyword
- How many books are competing for that keyword

With the category feature KDP Rocket will quickly find pertinent and niche categories for your books, as well as find out how many books you'd need to sell that day in order to be the new #1 bestseller. With this feature you'll discover:

- Niche categories to choose from
- Which categories will help you sell more books

- How many sales that day you'd need to make in order to be the new #1 bestseller
- How many sales you'd need to make in order to be listed in the top 20
- Learn About Other Authors & Their Sales

With a click of a button, you can see your potential competitors, their information, reviews, book cover, and even their daily and monthly earnings. By understanding what works for your competitors, you can create book titles, subtitles, and descriptions that convert better, increase your Kindle rankings, and sell more books.

KDP Rocket will help find you over 150 profitable keywords for your AMS book advertising campaign in under 10 seconds. Then, once you have your list of keywords, click export and upload it to AMS.

KDP Rocket is simple to use tool that works on both Mac and PC which basically does everything discussed above. The software is priced at $97, which I find is on the upper end of all the tested tools. You can try it free for 30 days and see if it works for you.

Here is the direct link to KDP Rocket: KDP Rocket

Find Keywords using MerchantWords

This is my favorite tool to find relevant keywords. It's a massive database (above 100 Million) of amazon keywords that are related to product sales. It's as simple as entering a phrase, and you will get all related keywords.

MerchantWords claims that they are using the most accurate, extensive, up-to-date collection of global shopper keyword search data available today. They have over one billion unique search phrases collected from Amazon shopper searches around the world.

That's one billion insights on consumer demand and shopping trends.

The way searches are done in one country are not always the same in another, and when you choose the right search terms your products are seen by more buyers. That goes for languages, too. MerchantWords gives you instant access to a global audience with a database of search terms from buyers in North America, Europe, Australia and Asia.

Collecting billions of keywords isn't easy, but the real work comes in understanding what keywords to use and when to use them. Their proprietary algorithm uses artificial intelligence to do the heavy lifting so you don't have to worry about it.

They monitor the Amazon search bar for actual shoppers' searches. This allows them to quickly spot trends and see what's in the minds of your potential customers. Using data science and proprietary algorithms, they compare all of the keywords that show up every time when they gather new data against the historical search terms in their database.

They also state that they are calculating and processing more than five years of keyword data – one billion unique keywords – and billions of signals from Amazon search results pages. These calculations allow them to organize and rank every keyword found on Amazon every month from 1 to 131,728,810 and counting – and that's just the U.S. results for the month of June 2018!

Taking into account the number of monthly Amazon shopper visits, they then allocate the proportional search volume across all search phrases. They repeat this process many times every month to provide the most up-to-date information available.

They also regularly run spot checks with Amazon sponsored advertising pay-per-click (PPC) search impression data, since that gives them a baseline readings for how many searches to expect for a keyword. While impressions are critical data points, they're just a portion of the overall volume and not a full measure of consumer demand.

I just found out that they have upgraded their system with some amazing new features. There are two new columns added to the search result.

Depth

This point system indicates how quickly a keyword appears when a user types in a search query in the Amazon search bar. The number displayed is on a scale of 1-25, with 1 representing the fastest and 25 representing the slowest. Keywords with a depth of 1 are likely to be very competitive. Keyword depth can vary based on search trends, algorithm changes, seasonality, and new product releases.

Seasonality

This column indicates how often a keyword is searched throughout the year. Keywords can be classified as evergreen: The keyword appears in search every month. Seasonal: The keyword has only appeared in a search for up to 3 months, no more. And New:

The keyword just appeared in search results. This column is still in the beta phase, and they are working to refine the results in the next few weeks.

Their service costs $30 if you only go for the US market, which is the biggest. I was able to negotiate an arrangement with MerchantsWords, and with my discount link, (not an affiliate link) you only pay $9 per month!

Here is the discount link to MerchantWords:
https://www.merchantwords.com/bookadreport

I highly recommend that you sign up for a month and use that time to research your keywords and build several ad campaigns. Here is a list of suggestions:

- Use related author names
- Use related titles or phrases from that title
- Use keywords that describe your genre
- Use genre keywords

After you put these phrases into MerchantWords, use the suggested lists and build your own keyword list. Make sure you are using the filter at the top and select Books from the categories. Use the estimated monthly search volume to filter out phrases that get below 1000 searches per month.

When you use broad keywords in your search, you may end up with a massive list of keywords. You can then drill even deeper into the results by selecting one of the broad keywords and receive a new, more detailed and long tail keyword list.

Find Keywords with ParseHub

Parsehub is a tool that supports complex data extraction from websites. It is equipped with machine learning technology that can read and analyze documents on the web to output relevant data. Parsehub is available as a desktop client for Windows, Mac, and Linux and there is also a web app that you can use within the browser. You can have up to 5 crawl projects with the free plan from Parsehub.

ParseHub is from its functionality a web scraper. There are about 7-10 other web scrapers; however I found that ParseHub is a breeze to learn and very easy to use once you understand how it works.

What does Web Scraping mean?

Web scraping is a term for various methods used to collect information from across the Internet. Generally, this is done with software that simulates human Web surfing to collect specified bits of information from different websites. Those who use web scraping programs may be looking to collect certain data to sell to other users, or to to use for promotional purposes on a website. [18]

Web scraping is essentially a form of data mining. Items like weather reports, auction details, market pricing, or any other list of collected data can be sought in web scraping efforts.

We will use web scraping to collect keywords, especially author names, titles and category names. The free version allows us to have five projects, which is enough, as we do not need to save them. After collecting keyword data, we can export them into a CSV or Excel format.

Using ParseHub is a bit more challenging than other tools because you need to download and install the program first on your computer. Then you need to create an account, and after that, you need a little practice time to understand how this program works.

We will use ParseHub in the following example to extract keywords from GoodReads Listopia. However, before we start let me explain a bit about GoodReads and Listopia.

Using GoodReads for Keywords

Goodreads is a social network specifically for authors and readers. It has over 20 million members and is one of the most visited websites in the world. It helps people find the next book they want to read. If you don't use GoodReads, please sign up for free and start listing your books there.

Goodreads has a feature called Listopia where people publicly vote on the top books on all manner of lists. This is the place where we can extract hundreds of relevant keywords.

So, let's get started.

I am using ,Best Science Fiction & Fantasy Books' as an example. You can use any list you want. In this example, we will extract the author and the title of the first 100 entries of this list. You can extract the entire list, of course, but it requires a bit more knowledge of how ParseHub works, and it would exceed the scope of this book.

There are plenty of training videos on their website that shows you all kind of scenarios and how to work with them. For example how to extract information from different pages at once. Most lists use page navigation to split long lists into several pages. ParseHub can automatically scrap information from one page, then skip over to the next page, and then start again until the end of the list.

Please follow these steps to learn from this example:

1. Download ParseHub from here.

2. Sign up for a free account

3. Open the application and click the green button ‚New Project

4. Go to GoodReads list and select a list from the tags on the right

5. Copy the URL you see in your browser

6. Paste the URL into the project field

7. Click on ‚Start Project on this URL'

8. Go to the right panel and select the first book title, then the second

9. Then click on the first author, then the second

10. Click on the green button ‚Get Data'

You are almost done!

Now you can either go for a Test Run or hit Run and let the program work. It will take a few minutes, depending on your Internet connection speed and the size of the list.

When your data is ready, you can download it with a click in either CSV, Excel or JSON format. I always use CSV because I can open it either with Excel, Apple numbers or with a simple text editor.

It's best you open it with Excel or any other spreadsheet program. If you do not have Excel, you can use Google's free Sheets program.

In your downloaded list, you will see now all titles and authors listed. Think about how much time you would need to do this manually.

How to use ParseHub Results?

Now, that you have a list of authors and titles that relate to your book genre or category you can use it to target your in an ad. Before you do that I want to give you a few hints on how to clean up that list.

In your downloaded Excel sheet, you will see three columns, the author name, the title, and the URL. You can delete the URL because it has no value for us. Now you can copy the column with all the authors and paste it into a new keyword campaign. Look at the author names, and if they have a letter for the middle name, delete it and then add that author name again. Most people will not search with a middle name that only contains a letter, e.g. Mike L. Hunt.

Go over the titles and use them right away if they are no longer than five words and don't contain any extra information. In all other cases extract phrases of the title people may use to search for the book. In most cases that would be the beginning of the title. Add these to your list, and you now have a targeted list of related keywords.

Now, when someone pulls up a book title from this list, your sponsored ad appears. It is highly likely that a reader gets a bit sidetracked and looks at other books on this page and find yours. That's basically how you set up and use these ads.

That was just one example of how to use the powerful feature of ParseHub. You can use it wherever a website contains lists of data. Amazon itself also works excellent. For example on your own dedicated book page you could extract author title and title from the following sections:

- Customers who bought this item also bought
- Sponsored products related to this item

Get Visual - Find Keywords with Yasiv

YASIV is a visual recommendation service that helps people find the right product from Amazon's catalog; be it a book, a movie or a video game. A link between the two products means that they are often bought together. By simply observing the network of products one can guess at what is popular and what isn't.

On almost every product, Amazon lists related items under "Customers Who Bought This Item Also Bought." Unfortunately, scrolling through that list and opening each item up is annoying.

YASIV gives you a tree spreading out from one item, showing you not just what other customers bought with that item, but what other customers bought from those result-ing items as well, giving you a massive web of books, albums, or anything else you might be interested in.

Go over to yasiv.com and use either your book title, your name or any phrase you like to start a search. On the right side, you will see the results coming in. The list length depends on how broad your search phrase is.

Once you have the list you can sort it by:

- Popularity
- Price
- Sales Rank
- Publication Date
- Number of Pages
- Pagerank

In the list, you can click on any title and see some more facts, which you can sort by. However, there is another exciting detail there, and these are tags. I just searched for my name and got a list of 415 books. Then I listed it by sales rank and Bob Woodward's book Fear came up on #3.

Her are the tags from that book:

- U.S. Presidents
- Hoaxes & Deceptions
- Russian & Former Soviet Union
- Executive Branch
- National & International Security

Use these tags as keywords if your title falls into the same category. You can use MerchantWords or any other keyword suggestion program to get further related keywords.

Now, how do you extract the whole list? Use ParseHub to get a list of all 415 titles. You can then maybe use only the first 100 regarding sales rank.

Here is how you do it:

- Load ParseHub and start a new project
- Copy and paste the URL from Yasiv into your project field

On the next screen click the Browse button on top. This tells ParseHub that you are not marking any data the program should extract. You need this because Yasiv gives you a Google Captcha to solve by clicking on it.

Once you have done that you will see the Yasiv web interface working its way to gather the list of books based on the phrase you had put in.

When the list is finished click on the ParseHub Browse button again to tell the program that you are now marking data to be used for extraction. Click on the first title and then click on the second title.

If you have a long list of books, in our case 415, your browser may give you are warning message that a script is not responding. If that happens, click on Continue to let the script finish. After a while, the program has collected all 415 titles, and you can now hit the ‚Get Data‘ button and as the last step save your list in CSV or Excel format.

How to Find the Best Categories?

Now, that we have covered the critical topic of keywords, there is another significant aspect of getting your book the best exposure. It is the book category you have or will choose when you first set up your book with KDP.

You are allowed to choose up to two categories, and you should use both of them. There is a simple way to add up to six other categories, and I will get to it later. For now, let's focus on how to find and choose a suitable category.

In the Kindle and book store together there are currently over 22.000 categories. These are not all available to the reader, which makes it a bit harder to find and dig them out.

Reasons why your book should have best fitting categories:

It can support you to become a bestseller in your genre. Amazon can tag your book with an orange badge that says ‚#1 Bestseller'. By appearing in different categories, your book can appeal to different audiences. If your book ranks in the top ten of any category listings, Amazon will include your book to its ‚Recommendations Engine' which will generate more publicity! [19]

How should I choose categories?

Choose the most accurate categories based on the subject matter of your book. Avoid choosing one category that's explicitly fiction and another that's explicitly non-fiction. Also, select specific categories instead of general ones. Customers looking for particular topics will find your book more easily. Amazon will display your book in the general categories as well. Choose a ‚General‘ category only if your book is a general book about a broad topic.

Choosing a single category will display your book in a variety of searches, so don't list your book in a category and its sub-categories. One specific, accurate category is more effective than a redundant second one.

Find out which categories are the best fit for your book. Search for categories on Amazon. Look for relevant browse categories on the left under the Kindle Store > Kindle eBooks header. You can also search for books like yours and find the browse categories assigned to those books.

Kindle Categories with Keyword Requirements

To list your book in specific sub-categories on Amazon.com and Amazon.co.uk, you'll need to add search keywords to the categories you choose. You will find a table with all the required keywords in the FAQ section of the Kindle direct publishing guidelines on Amazon. I have the link also added in the resource section of this book.

How to Acquire Additional Categories

When you upload your book for the first time, Amazon will present you with a list of categories to choose from. You will notice that the selection is limited and is lacking many categories you may have seen other book listed by. Amazon has done this intentionally so that they can place new books into their own Kindle categories.

You can contact Amazon and request your book to be placed in a distinct category. They will assess your book and determine if it's an appropriate fit for the specific browse category. If they approve it, your book will be listed in this category as well. [20]

Categories and Your Ranking Potential

Adding your book to the right category influences the probability to get the ‚#1 Best Seller' badge. Having this badge right beneath your ratings is a big buying influencer. Once in a while, I get this badge for one of my books, and I always observe that the sales go up about 20-30%.

Every category needs a certain amount of sales to get to the top and receive the best-seller badge. Go to the Kindle store select a category that interests you. Then choose a book of the list, but do not choose one of the sponsored books at the top. When you are on the designated book description page scroll down to where you see Product details.

At the bottom of this list, you will see Amazon Best Sellers Rank. There you will see the rank of the book in the Kindle store, e.g. #804 Paid in Kindle Store. Below you will find up to three categories where this book is ranked. It used to show the complete path with the main and subcategories. As I am writing this Amazon seems to make adjustments to this section, and I have seen only the subcategory without the complete path. I don't know if this will stay or not.

Click on the first entry at the end where you see the last sub category. This may look like this:

#10 in Kindle Store > Kindle eBooks > Science Fiction & Fantasy > Science Fiction > **First Contact**

#11 in Books > Science Fiction & Fantasy > Science Fiction > **First Contact**

#13 in Kindle Store > Kindle eBooks > Science Fiction & Fantasy > Fantasy > **Coming of Age**

In this case it would be ‚First Contact'. This will bring you to an overview page where Amazon lists ‚Best Sellers in First Contact Science Fiction eBooks'. Continue, and click on the first title, which is the bestseller in this category. This will bring up the dedicated book page and you will see that this book has the badge ‚#1 Best Seller'. Scroll down as before to the ‚Product details' until you see the Amazon Best Seller Rank. Next to it you will see the rank that is required for this category to be number one!

In this case I see a number of 184, which tells me that this book sells like hot cookies. I have included a list that shows you the Amazon ranks and how it equates into book sales. This table[21] reflects only an estimate, because it does not account for borrows and Kindle Unlimited. Dave Chessen, from Kindlepreneur [22] also offers a nice sales estimate calculator on his website, and you will find the link is in the resource section.

Please use this table only as a raw estimate!

Amazon Sales Rank - Sold Books per Day

- Rank 50,000 to 100,000 - 1 book
- Rank 10,000 to 50,000 - 5 to 15 books
- Rank 5,500 to 10,000 - 15 to 25 books
- Rank 3,000 to 5,500 - 25 to 70 books
- Rank 1,500 to 3,000 - 70 to 100 books
- Rank 750 to 1,500 - 100 to 120 books
- Rank 500 to 750 - 120 to 175 books
- Rank 350 to 500 - 175 to 200 books
- Rank 200 to 350 - 200 to 300 books
- Rank 35 to 200 - 300 to 1,000 books
- Rank 20 to 35 - 1,000 to 2,000 books
- Rank of 5 to 20 - 2,000 to 3,000 books
- Rank of 1 to 5 - 3,000+ books

Use Kindle Spy to Find the Best Categories

Finding a good category this way is time-consuming and not very efficient. Luckily there are many people that have faced the same problem, and some of them have come up with automated tools or entire programs.

The best program and the one I used to get one of my books into the bestseller category is KDSpy or KindleSpy.

The program integrates directly into your browser. That means you can do your research right on Amazon. It uncovers hot niche opportunities on Kindle. While browsing the Kindle marketplace, the program will analyze the bestseller categories behind the scenes and have the essential data you need to reverse-engineer the bestseller categories, search results, and author pages.

When you want a detailed breakdown of any Kindle or Book category on Amazon, you'll know the competitor landscape of that category, the potential estimated profit you could make there with a first-page listing. It will also show you a detailed breakdown of each book's performance.

Once you've identified an ideal category, you can reveal the estimated daily sales you'll need for Amazon's algorithm to pay attention to your book – highlighting how to rank #1 and #20 in any given Kindle or book category.

What better way to find bestselling niches – and get ideas for your next book – than by modeling what's already working for other top authors. This browser extension shows you the hot trends in any market, reveals the bestselling niches to go after – and even gives you a word cloud to help you write a compelling book title.

KDSPY can also analyse any author page and tell you in seconds all their statistics. Just a single click will show you the SalesRank of all their Kindle, Paperback & Hardcover books, their estimated sales, and total revenues broken down by individual book type.

Keep track of as many Kindle, Paperback & Hardcover books as you'd like with the included book tracking feature. It pulls the SalesRank of your competitor's books and displays their rank in chart form along with their estimated daily sales averaged out over the month.

I found that the tracking stats only go back for 30 days. I wished that would be at least 90 days or even longer. Also, the updating of reviews and other facts are sometimes lagging at least a month if not longer. Despite these disadvantages the program does what it claims and finding lucrative categories is now a breeze.

Using the program requires a one-time payment of $47. It can help you find the right categories for your book. Listing your book in the right category is the foundation of your book's success. With this program, you can do in minutes, what used to be many clicks and hours of work.

Here is the link to KDSpy: KDSpy - Find Lucrative Kindle Niches

Chapter 5 - Writing Successful Ads

What Makes a Good Ad?

I am not going to make this a long chapter. I was even considered to leave it out. There are plenty of great websites available that explain advertising in general. Just do a Google search on it.

However, it belongs to the pool of facts that make or break your ad campaign. Therefore, I will give you a few hints and tips on how to make the most of the 120 characters you have available for your Amazon keyword ads. Besides that, I will also explain a few relevant facts on how to write a good book description.

Making the Most out of 150 Characters

For a Sponsored product ad Amazon allows you to use up to 150 characters. That's not a lot, so you should use this space very wisely. For an ad to be effective, you need to have a clear intention of what you want to achieve.

If you want to get to the core of advertising read his book[23] ‚The Adweek Copywriting Handbook: The Ultimate Guide to Writing Powerful Advertising and Marketing Copy from One of America's Top Copywriters'. He is known throughout the advertising world as a copywriting legend and role model. His ads have moved millions of customers to reach for their wallets.

Joseph Sugarman described the goal of writing effective advertising copy as being: ‚To cause a person to exchange his or her hard-earned money for a product or service'. Your ad needs to trigger any form of action by the reader.

To inspire action, you need to create desire.[24] You accomplish this by making a powerful offer that appeals first to the emotional, and second to the logical side of the reader.

Shoppers on Amazon click your ad because they want to accomplish something and solve a problem. Because of this reason, one of the most effective copywriting strategies is to mirror the user's goal in your ad copy. When you write your ads, think of the user and what they want to accomplish – then convey your ads in a way that directly appeals to this desire.[25] Desire is partly driven by needs, and who better than Maslow's explained the hierarchy of human needs.

Maslow's Hierarchy of Needs

American psychologist Maslow argued that human behaviour is always the result of one (or more) of the five basic human needs, such as:

- Physiological needs – hunger, thirst, shelter, clothing and sex
- Safety – the need for physical, emotional and financial security
- Social needs – the need for love and belonging
- Esteem – need for achievement, care and respect
- Self-actualization – the need to achieve one's own full potential

Successful advertising should address at least one of these five needs, in order to meet the user's needs, desires and aspirations.

Create Emotional Triggers

Nothing motivates people into action like a powerful emotional response. People read something, experience a strong emotional reaction to it, and then click. This technique is one of the most powerful skills you have when writing your 150 character ad.

Be very careful with negative emotions, such as anger, disgust, and fear as they can provoke a powerful response in the reader. It's difficult and also challenging to follow through with your book description. It's true that 90% of people are more focused on avoiding something than on accomplishing something. In other words, people mostly trying to avoid fear and loss, instead of focusing on creating.

Positive emotional triggers, such as affirmation and humor, can be highly effective at in your ads – especially these days where we all surrounded by a massive flood of negative news. Humour is a fantastic tool to get the readers attention, and it's easy to follow through with your book description.

Focus on the Benefits

Sadly, we live in an increasingly selfish society. Nobody cares about why your book is supposedly awesome.[26] The shopper only cares about how you can make their lives easier. To find at least one benefit is easy if you have a non-fiction book. However, what is the benefit of my science fiction novel? Well, for starters how about entertainment? How about the benefit to give your reader a short break from their daily working routine. With your book, your reader may relax into another world, that provides them with amusement, pleasure, relaxation and even inspiration.

Include Your Keywords

Don't make your prospects guess what book you are trying to sell. Make the connection between your book by including at least one keyword or a phrase in your ad text. If the shopper looks for ‚science fiction time travel' why not give the reader the impression that they have found something that they are looking for?

This is even more important if your book content is non-fiction.

Ask Questions

Leveraging user intent is crucial to increase conversion rates. Posing a question in your ad can lead to an immediate response - in the form of an answer - in the mind of the shopper. When you follow up your ad text or your book description with an answer well, you are riding along the same path with your shopper. Your book title may even include the answer the reader is looking for.

Include Numbers or Statistics

Many readers respond well to empirical evidence. Hard data can be a trust signal, and it can plant the seed of trustworthiness in the mind of your future reader. Psychologically, people are naturally drawn to numerals more than words.

Numbers take up less space than words that reflect the same values. Numbers also represent facts, so they naturally attract people who are searching for concrete information. If you can assign a specific number to your claims, your ad will come across as much more authoritative.

Odd numbers seem to connect better with readers over even numbers. This is because odd numbers are seen as more authentic than even numbers. Just make sure to only write with them when it works to your advantage.[27]

Some of the Best Ad Copy Ever

Look at these 50 ad copy headlines and get inspired. They have been the most successful ad copy in history [28]. Not all of them may be usable anymore, but they may give you an idea or a direction where you could go with your ad.

1. How I Made a Fortune With a Fool Idea
2. Thousands Have This Priceless Gift – but Never Discover It!
3. Six Types of Investors – Which Group Are You In?

4. Does Your Child Ever Embarrass You?

5. To People Who Want To Write – but Can't Get Started

6. The Crimes We Commit Against Our Stomachs

7. Dare To Be Rich!

8. How To Rob Banks Legally

9. A Startling Fact About Money

10. How To Discover What You Are Really Good At

11. How To Write a Business Letter

12. The Secrets of Making People Like You

13. Advice to Wives Whose Husbands Don't Save Money

14. How a New Discovery Made a Plain Girl Beautiful

15. How to Win Friends and Influence People

16. How to Swim with The Sharks without Being Eaten Alive

17. Do You Make This Mistakes in English?

18. Why Some Foods "Explode" in Your Stomach

19. You Can Laugh at Money Worries – if You Follow This Simple Plan

20. How I Improved My Memory in One Evening

21. Suppose This happened On Your Wedding Day!

22. The Secret to Being Wealthy

23. Imagine Holding an Audience Spellbound for 30 Minutes

24. Why Wall Street Journal readers Live Better

25. You May Be Eating More Salt Than You Should

26. Get Rid of That Humidity!

27. How To Get More Energy From The Food You Eat

28. They Grinned When the waiter Spoke to Me in French

29. How I Improved Memory in One Evening

30. Get Rid of Money Worries for Good

31. Keep Your Dog safe This Summer!

32. The Instrument of the Immortals
33. For People Who Don't Have Time for Unimportant Books
34. How To Avoid Mental Hazards
35. Break Out of Jail!
36. Will You Help me Free Gina?
37. Don't Even Think About Buying New Home Without Reading This Report!
38. How To Start from Scratch and Become a PO Box Millionaire
39. The Secret of Having Good Luck
40. How To Get Rich Reading Classified Ads
41. Seven Steps to Financial Freedom
42. How To Write a Hit Song and Sell It
43. How The Experts Buy and Sell Gold and Silver
44. Want to Be a Legal Investigator?
45. How To Write a Good Advertisement
46. Give Back What They Deserve
47. How To Burn Off Body Fat, Hour-by-Hour
48. Why Some People Almost Always Make Money in The Stock Market?
49. How Much is Your Working "Tension" Costing Your Company?
50. 161 New Ways to a Man's Heart – in This fascinating Book
51. Little Leaks That Keep Men Poor
52. This is Marie Antoinette – Riding To Her Death
53. Take This One Minute Test!
54. The Truth About Getting Rich
55. Do Your Employees Work as Slowly as They read?
56. The Most Expensive Mistake of Your Life
57. 7 ways to Collect Your Unpaid Bills
58. What Your Lawyer Doesn't Want You to Know

Here is what Amazon thinks you should do with your ad: 'Make sure your ad copy describes what you're selling, but add humor and creativity when appropriate. Standing out in the eyes of your customers is crucial in the massive Amazon search results, and a little urgency in the text never hurt.'

Here is a summary of what we discussed. As mentioned before, it presents just a few general guidelines for crafting your ad copy. However, you may already get the essence of it. Otherwise, please pick up a good book on advertising in general or google some specific questions you may have. Also, please look at the resource section where you will find a few recommendations on good books and websites.

- Be clear about your main benefit
- Announce exciting news
- Use questions
- Appeal to you reader's hunger for knowledge
- Tell your audience what to do
- Create the most valuable information resource
- Surprise them
- Elicit curiosity
- Give how to advice
- Use numbers and statistics
- Say it simply and directly

What You Should Avoid

Amazon has some specific requirements when it comes to the text you use in your ads. Make sure you are not using one of the topics outlined below; otherwise your ad may get rejected.

- Must not contain any additional unnecessary information or foul, vulgar, or obscene language, including censored words that indicate foul, vulgar, or obscene language

- Must not contain special characters or symbols, including legal symbols (for example, ©)

- Must not end with article words (e.g., "Last of the Mohicans, The")

- Must match the title and author text displayed in the image, and accurately represent the product being advertised

- Must not end with any punctuation marks other than a single question or exclamation mark

- Ad copy cannot be in ALL CAPS, unless the book cover or title on the detail page is formatted in the same way, or for well-known abbreviations such as YA (Young Adult)

- Does not contain any pricing messages

- Does not present customers with emotionally draining or depressing messages

- Does not contain customer reviews, unless the specific review is contained in the book description on the detail page

- Does not contain third-party customer reviews or rating scores, third-party editorial reviews are acceptable

- Does not refer to the Amazon rating score

- Does not use overly forceful phrases or exclamation points (e.g. "Don't miss out!", "HURRY – SAVE NOW" are not acceptable)

- Does not contain any special offers, promotions or contests

Ad Copy Success Words

There is plenty of data available on what makes a great Google ad. I know, that's an entirely different platform. However, there is some common ground here that I want to share with you. Google Ads have expanded their ad format in recent years and allow up to 140 characters. That's very close to the 150 characters Amazon keyword-based ads allow.

When it comes to high click-through rates, there are a few keywords that seem to trigger more click responses than others. You may want to take a second look at the list with the 50 best ad copy ever. What you will discover is a set of keywords that appear over and over.

Words sell!

They always have and they probably always will - especially in the media-driven world, which is still primarily text-based. There is a huge trend in the last years that shifts away from text-based ads into video ads on the Internet. No wonder, as more and more people have access to high-speed, broadband Internet connection. However, as long as Amazon offers ads that can add up to 150 characters, we still want to make the most out of this 150 characters.

Let's take a look at the most powerful words[29] you could use in your ad.

1. Power Word - Now

Yes, it has been overused and is slowly beginning to lose its power. However, it is still working. It creates the feeling that I must act urgently to take advantage of an offer.

This is connected with the underlying fear not to lose something that could ensure my survival. It also implies the possibility of instant gratification.

2. Power Word - Easy

It is ingrained in the human consciousness not to do any hard work if there is an easier way. The concept of ease and speed is based on the attempt to accomplish any task most efficiently. Therefore, I always consider the option to do things without additional effort. Be careful, because this word is also overused. Make sure if you use it, you can deliver on your promise, e.g. ‚Build your house in three easy steps‘.

3. Power Word - Free

If I want to buy a product, I don't want to take a financial risk. Handing my money over in exchange for a product where I don't know if it works for me can create financial stress. Therefore, I lean towards a positive reaction when I see something is offered for free. Any dissatisfaction with the purchased product will not lead to financial imbalance.

4. Power Word - New

Most of us want something new because new means it's better. It could be improved or look nicer. Neurologists studies found that the quest of novelty is submerged deep in our consciousness. New things activate the center for rewards in the human brain, which may be correspondent to several millennia of development of human civilization and the constant effort for progress and improvement.

5. Power Word - You

When your ad text contains the word ‚You‘, it is personal, because it speaks directly to the reader. It addresses a person's desire, needs, passion, personal problems, offers solutions for a personal dilemma. Everyone wants a product that is made exactly for them, for his or her likes, tastes and habits. When the message of an ad speaks directly to me I feel chosen, picked and selected. It's like the experience to be in a store, where the clerk hands me over a product - I was not even aware of - that I was looking for.

Last, but not least a few more words that originated from print ads, but are used as well in online advertising. I am closing this chapter with an expanded list of power words, which are also most frequently used and have proven to be very successful.

The Top 20 Print Media Adjectives

New, Good/Better/Best, Free, Fresh, Delicious, Full (Fully), Sure, Clean, Wonderful, Special, Crisp, Fine, Big, Great, Real, Easy, Bright, Extra, Safe and Rich.[30]

Forty-Eight Power Words

This list, originally complied by Linda Roth and Curtis Circulation Company, was derived from best-selling magazine covers. Interweave's Bob Kaslik determined that it works equally well in promo copy and email subject lines.

Improve, Trust, Immediately, Discover, Profit, Learn, Know, Understand, Powerful, Best, Win, Hot Special, More, Bonus, Exclusive, Extra, You, Free, Health, Guarantee, New, Proven, Safety, Money, Now, Today, Results, Protect, Help, Easy, Amazing, Latest, Extraordinary, How to, Worst, Ultimate, Hot, First, Big, Anniversary, Premiere, Basic, Complete, Save, Plus!, Create.[31]

Optimising Your Book Description

The book description is the main pitch to your reader about why they should buy your book. It is a sales copy to get them to see that the book is for them and then make the purchase.

Start with the hook. The first sentence should be something that will grab the attention of your reader and make them take notice. You need to get that right; otherwise you may lose the reader immediately. After that, it doesn't matter what the rest of your book description says.[32]

Sadly, most people these days have an attention span of less than a few seconds. They are easily distracted and always looking for a reason to move on to the next thing. Make the first sentence something that glues their attention, and to read the rest of your book description. Every good book description is interesting from the first sentence.

This means you should focus on the boldest claim in the book, or the most impressive fact, or the most compelling idea. What's just popping into your mind is most likely exactly that.

Once you have their attention, then clearly describe the current discomfort or trouble they may in. If you can accurately and realistically portray the stress and pressure, maybe also the pain of the reader, you will have them fully engaged in the description, and at this point, they are seriously entertaining the idea of buying your book.

- What unsolved problems do they have?
- What unachieved aspirations and goals do they have?

Clearly and directly express these in plain and simple language.

In the next step tell your reader what your book does to help them solve this discomfort, stress, irritation or pain. When this is done right, it creates an emotional connection by describing how your book will make the reader feel after reading it. What's even better is when the reader understands what they will get out of reading the book.

- Will it make them happy or rich?
- Will it help them lose weight or have more friends?
- What do they get once they read this book?

Be precise about the benefits, don't suggest or indicate things to them. You are selling a result to the reader, which is delivered through reading your book. Explain exactly what the book is about, in clear, unmistakable terms.

Let them know that you are an authority in your field. Let the reader understand why they should listen to you. Explain in simple words why you are the expert that they need to hear from. This should be very short and should not take the focus of the book description. Give your reader just enough social proof to make them keep reading.

This social proof or the facts why you are an authority could also go at the beginning of your book description, where we started with a hook. If you managed to be on the NYT Bestseller list before with one of your books, then you should mention this fact in the first sentence (maybe even in bold).

Keep the loop open. When you state the problem or the question your book addresses, you show that you can solve or answer it. However, make sure you leave a crucial small piece out. This piques the interest of the reader and leaves them wanting more - sort of cliffhanger. Don't be too explicit about what they will learn. You don't have have to go deep into the how you solve the reader's pain or problem. If you spill all the beans why would the reader continue and buy your book?

Don't make the reader guess what your point is. This is especially true for prescriptive books like how-to, self-help, motivational, etc. [33]

Book Description Best Practices

Don't think of your book description is a synopsis. It's not meant to summarise your book. Resist that urge to put everything about your book in this section.

Your book description is an advertisement. It's like a movie trailer for an upcoming new release. Its purpose is to make people want to read your book. You want them to take action and buy it.

Use compelling keywords that you may have used for your ad already. Take a look at the previous section to get a feel of good keywords. Also, think about keywords that are frequently searched. When you include high traffic keywords, it will increase the possibility that your book will get picked up in Amazon's search.

Don't go to the maximum length if you think you are done. Keep it short and simple. The average Amazon Bestsellers have a descriptions length around 200 words. Most descriptions are broken up into several paragraphs. You can use basic HTML formatting options like bold, italic, line break, and bullets.

Again, keep your writing simple and use short, clear sentences. Don't force your reader to struggle and comprehend what you're trying to say because you've strung too many ideas together in one long run-on sentence.

Always write as the publisher and not as the author!

It's maybe obvious to you, but the book description should always be in a third person objective voice, and never your author voice. It is always written as someone else describing your book.

Be very careful by comparing your book to other books. It may cause the book and you to look inferior. There is also a chance that your reader may dislike the book you are comparing yourself. It just takes a second for your reader to move away from your book description.

Consider the idea that you let someone else write the book description for you. You, as the author is often the worst choice to write the book description. You may be too close to the material and also emotionally invested. Ask a friend to help, or go to a professional editor or even better, a professional copywriter, for assistance.

The last step in your book description should be the Call To Action (CTA). You are finally telling the reader nicely what to do. Your reader just finished reading the last sentence of your book description. Now, your job is to tease them. Remind them they can have even more thrills, insights and solutions if they buy your book!

Make sure you are using third person, present tense. Your blurb should sound like someone describing the book, face to face.

Chapter 6 - Testing & Optimising

How Do I Improve My ROI?

Once you have started with advertising on Amazon, you need to be patient. Most of our ads won't have 100 clicks per day, where you can begin optimizing already after a few days. In my experience ads need to run at least 4-6 weeks until you can make adjustments to them.

You need to have at least 100 clicks before you start optimizing; otherwise you don't have meaningful data.

When you optimize a Sponsored Product ad with keywords, your first step is to check what keywords have gotten any clicks or sales. Got to your advertising dashboard and click on the ad you want to optimize. You will see your table with keywords. All the header columns are sortable by simply clicking on them. Click them once to sort ascending and click them twice for sorting the rows in a descending way.

Let's first look what keywords got the most impressions. Click on the ‚Impr‘ header column twice to sort the keywords by impressions.

Weeding Out - Looking at Impressions

If you see any keywords at the top that have more than 3000 impressions and no click, you should pause them. Amazon doesn't let you delete these keywords, only allows you to pause them. These keywords don't attract people to your ad, and therefore you do no longer want them.

You may think, that even with no clicks, these non-performing keywords give you free exposure. Yes, that is true. However, it hurts your overall ad performance. Two things can happen if you have too many non-performing keywords in your ad campaign. First, as mentioned before, your overall ad performance goes down, and Amazon may show at one point in the future another ad instead, that performs better than yours. Second, you may risk that Amazon suspends your ad because of low relevancy.

To ensure an ad is both interesting to potential buyers and effective for you, Amazon actively compares it with similar ads to determine if it's relevant. Relevance is determined in part by customer click-through rates, so if too few customers are clicking an ad, the campaign can be stopped, and you will receive an email with suggestions on how to improve relevancy.

If your campaign is stopped, create a new campaign with an eye toward more specific interests and products your potential customer would likely have.

Let's continue with weeding out low performing keywords. After you paused the keywords with impressions above 3000 and no clicks, we want to look at keywords that got no impressions at all. Simply click on the ‚Impr' header column again, and the keywords are now sorted in descending way.

Pause all keywords that have less than 200 impressions and no click.

Weeding Out - Looking at Clicks

Now, we want to look at clicks and make improvements on keywords related to low and high performers. Click twice on the ‚Clicks' column header, and you should see keywords sorted that have the most clicks.

Next to the clicks column, you see the average cost per click, and right next to it the summary of your ad spending for that particular keyword. As a first step, we want to look at keywords with many clicks and no sales. If your average cost per click is between 30-50 cents, and your ad spend is above $3 then I would suggest lowering the bid for this keyword by at least 50%.

Those keywords may appeal to your reader, but for some reason, they do not convert to sales at your dedicated book page. The title and description of your book may not match this keyword. People got interested, clicked and wanted to know more, but couldn't.

At one point in the future, you may pause this keyword. However, for right now, and as a first step, just lower the bid.

Moving on, we want to go in the other direction and increase the bid for keywords that do perform well. To get there, please click twice on the last column ‚ACoS'. This will show you the best performing keywords.

We talked already about how to calculate your break-even ACoS. Look at the numbers and focus on all keywords that show a lower value than your calculated break-even number. Now, look at the ‚ACPC' and your bid amount. The bid amount should be at least 25-50% higher than what you see at the ‚ACPC'.

If that's not the case, please change the bid and increase it by 25-50%. You can do this by clicking on the bid, edit the number and click save. Repeat this with all keywords which fall under this radar.

Congratulations, you just optimised your ad campaign!

Please have an eye on your optimized ad campaign as often as you can. Depending on the number of clicks you get, maybe even daily. Yes, this is time-consuming! However, there is a solution to automate this step.

I have developed a program called ‚Book Ad Report' that has a build in ‚Keyword Optimiser' tool. I was as frustrated as many other authors with the insufficient campaign statistic that Amazon provides. As you may know, the stats are accumulated over time and don't allow you to go back in time. It's almost impossible to compare campaign data between weeks or days, without having the Excel data saved each day, and next to each other.

That's where I started to develop a program that could compare the data and provide me with meaningful charts and data. To make a long story short, this little program grew up over time and has become now a service platform. Book Ad Report was developed to turn these plain ad campaign tables into meaningful and delicious charts, with the ability to select a particular time frame and see how your ads performed.

Using the build in ‚Keyword Optimiser‘ you upload your campaign stats and campaign keywords, and it will run a diagnostic on it. The result is a five-step optimization suggestion, which shows you in detail all the keywords that need optimization, and what needs to be optimized. Basically, every optimization step - and a few more - that I have shown you in this chapter.

I will get into more details about the Book Ad Report when we cover the topic of tracking your ads.

The calculations are based on over 100 campaigns for my own books, you may have to experiment with slightly different numbers depending on your book genre.

How Do I Scale My Ads?

Scaling your ads means you use what works and expand on it. By optimizing your ads - like what we did in the previous chapter - you are already working toward the direction of scaling your ads. However, you will soon realize that there is a limit on how far you can go by simply optimizing your ad.

To expand means to double, triple or even scale up your ads by the factor 10. If you have a successful ad that makes you $200 profit per months, it seems logical to expand that success to the level where you have $2000 profit.

Would you enjoy being a professional author, and drop the other work, you may only do to survive?

Remember the statistic I mentioned at the beginning of the book? A recent report from Data Guy and Hugh Howey's Author Earnings spots 'more than 4,600 authors earning $25,000 or above from their sales on Amazon.com.' "1,340 authors are earning $100,000 per year or more from Amazon sales. Half of them are indies and Amazon-imprint authors."

Again, once you have an ad that is successful, you can expand on it. Unfortunate, this is not as easy as it sounds. You need to broaden your advertising into other categories or book genres. Depending on your book genre this may be simple or difficult. I can only give you an example of how I did it.

I started advertising my book ,The Money Deception - What Banks & Governments Don't Want You to Know, by targeting keywords in the area:

- Banking
- Fraud
- Government
- Capitalism

I used the main keywords from my book title and description. In the beginning, this ad was filled with over 600 keywords!

What was I thinking?

I used all of these phrases, punched it into MerchantWords and exported the complete list. After about four weeks I started to optimize and tweak. Over 300 keywords had zero impressions, which I paused. Another 2-3 weeks and that ad was performing very well; however it was already close to peak performance regarding book sales.

Now was the time of brainstorming. What other market segments could I target with this book? Here is what I came up with:

- Top 100 financial books
- Consumerism
- Coverup
- White Collar Crime
- Austrian
- Crisis 2008
- Corruption
- Economics
- Economy
- Macroeconomics

- Debt
- History of Money
- Conspiracy

For each of these segments, I used MerchantWords and GoodReads Listopia to get a list of related keywords, author names and book titles. In your campaign overview use the copy function to create a new ad.

As a first step, edit the name of the ad and use your targeted market segment phrase to distingue it from the others. Then, import the keywords list, set your bid the same as the previous one, and as a last step revise your ad text to match the new market segment.

Let it run for 3-4 weeks and start optimizing it as I have explained before. You do this with every ad, until you have only successful ads running. Much work you may say. Yes, I wish it would be easier. However, when you stick with this formula, then you will succeed. I know from many authors that have started with Amazon advertising and gave up after a month or two.

One of the most important things I have learned from scaling ads is the ability to think outside the box. As an author, you most likely start with a very narrow view of what your audience may be. That's why it is essential for advertising, that you put your mind where your reader is. Ask your friends and even strangers about your book. Who do you think would be interested in reading this?

Also, use the free ‚Yasiv‘ tool I mentioned to find related books. Look at the books and then click on them to get to the dedicated Amazon page. Find the product details section and see in what category this book is listed. Sometimes you also find new ideas by reading the description of the book.

Chapter 7 - Tracking & Analysing

Tracking Ad Performance with Excel

Tracking your ads should be an essential part of your advertising planning. How do you know if you are making a profit with your ad campaign if you don't track the success? How can you make improvements to an ad if you don't know that it could perform 50% better? How do you compare the progress of your ads from the previous month to the actual month?

All of these questions need to be answered for you to make your advertising campaigns successful - and I mean all of your campaigns - not just a few of them.

As you may know, Amazon gives you only accumulated data. One of the most important numbers, of course, is your sales, spend and ACoS column. When you start these numbers increase slowly, and you may get a good feel by just looking at the numbers where you are with your sales, spend and ACoS. However, once you have 5-10 campaigns or even more running over a month time, you most likely lose the ability to make sense of the data Amazon shows you on your dashboard.

That's where the questions start to rise...

- How do I compare my clicks, sales and spend from one day to another?
- How did my ads perform last week?
- How is my ad campaign performing since I changed some of the bids?

Amazon does not provide any form of ad performance timeline. This was a shocking experience for me once I realized this. I used to spend $10.000 per month on Google Adwords about 7-8 years ago, and I could get very sophisticated analytical data back. Actually, the analytics tools were just short of overwhelming.

However, after a steep learning curve, I was able to tweak my ads several times and was able to make a good profit in a very competitive market. In the beginning, I lost money and without the detailed, and analytical tools Google provided I would not be able to be successful with my company.

Now, what do you do if you don't have these tracking tools? You have to create it on your own!

Fortunately, Amazon gives you the option to download your complete campaign dashboard in one file. There is an icon on the right top next to the dropdown option where you can choose the number of results per page. When you click this button, you can download a comma separated file (CSV), which contains all campaigns and all statistics for these campaign at the current time!

If you use Windows, you may have Microsoft Excel, and you can open this file. If you are using a Mac, you can use ‚Numbers' to open that file. In case you don't have any of these programs you can use the free Google sheets program.

For tracking purposes, you should rename this file and add the actual date to it. When you download this file, it is saved as ‚campaigns.csv'. Simply rename it to ‚campaigns-09-02-2018.csv', where 09-02-2018 would be the current date. It would be best if you did this around the same day at the same time.

Why?

Because this file represents the momentary status of all your campaigns! Amazon is updating the dashboard stats several times per day. If you want to compare data from one day to another, you should compare two files from the same time period. For example, you download it Monday evening at 08:00 and then again Tuesday evening around 8:00.

Don't worry about a few hours of difference. However, you won't get a good result if you download one campaign file on Monday evening and the next on following Tuesday morning.

To analyze your ad campaigns from two days, you load both campaigns files into Excel and compare each column from each campaign row with each other. You do this by subtracting the values in each cell from a particular day from the previous day.

This may look like the following:

- Monday Campaign 1 - Clicks 57
- Tuesday Campaign 1 - Clicks 64

Campaign 1 Clicks per day: 64-57 = 7

Let's say it is Thursday, and you have already your campaign file downloaded for Wednesday, then it may look like this:

- Tuesday Campaign 1 - Clicks 64
- Wednesday Campaign 1 - Clicks 70

Campaign 1 Clicks per day: 70-64 = 6

Do you see what we do here? We always deal with a set of accumulated numbers. Every day your columns will be higher than the day before. At least that's how it should be. If your ad does not get any impressions, clicks or sales than these numbers stay the same and your calculation will show zero for the day.

I may hear you saying: ‚Are you kidding me?‘ That's an awful time consuming and cumbersome way to track my ads. Yes, it is, and I wish Amazon would provide better analytical tools.

This is one of the reasons many people will give up because they don't have the time and patience to do this. Fortunately, that's an advantage for you if you stick with it because there is less competition around.

There are ways to program Excel to do some calculation between charts automatically for you, but this goes beyond what I want to cover in this book. Also, I have a big surprise for you in the next chapter, where I reveal a solution to this problem.

Tracking with BookAdReport.com

You may know that I am the author of over 20 books, and most of them cover the financial sector. What you probably don't know is that I am also a skilled programmer. I bought my first computer when I was 15 years old on a computer fair. It was a Sinclair ZX80. About the size of a large paperback book. Can you imagine - It had 4K of memory? That's about 4100 characters!

I used to be around computers from my early age, and every year a computer would get faster and more efficient and more powerful. Soon the Internet came into existence, and you could run programs on servers. A huge advantage, because theoretical anybody in the world would be able to access this program from home or work.

Let's fast forward to the year 2018, where the Internet has become the most potent communications instrument and also provides the most sophisticated tools. You have access now to information and programs that were unthinkable even ten years ago.

Once I started advertising with Amazon, I realized the problem with tracking, and as I already shared with you, that was also the reason I almost quit.

However, being an entrepreneur, you don't easily quit. I picked up where I left my ad campaigns and started all new. Guess what, that frustrating tracking issue hit me again. I started to download my campaign files every day around the same time and compared the results. I did this for about 2-3 weeks until the frustration level increased to the point where I needed a better solution.

I started to analyze the campaign file and programmed a simple tool that would read the file and store it into a database. One of the challenges was to figure out how to handle the date issue. Remember, the Amazon campaign file you download has no time or date stamps. There are only accumulated data available. However, these are the challenges that drive innovation forward, and after a few weeks of coding I had something very basic in functionality, and I could able to see the result of comparing two campaign files at a glance.

This was an exciting moment that helped me to get a ‚feel‘ how may ads were performing. I could see easily which ads performed well and which not. I could see my daily sales numbers!

Now, as an entrepreneur, I always think about how to make things better and make it available for other people. That's when the journey started to create a complete analytics ad campaign dashboard for Amazon book ads.

Again, fast forward to 2018 where I know write this book, this tool is ready for primetime and available for anybody. Here are just a few highlights of what you can do with the program.

Book Ad Report Features

Turn your plain amazon book campaigns into significant, delicious charts and see your ad campaign performance over selected time periods at a glance.

- Individual charts for Impressions, Clicks, CTR, Gross Sales, Ad Spending, CPC, ACoS, Campaign Sales, Sales Target and Ad Spending Target.
- Individual panels for Impressions, Clicks, CTR, Gross Sales, Ad Spending, CPC, ACoS, Campaign Sales, Average ACoS, Average CTR, Average Sales per day.

Customisable & Flexible

Each chart and panel can be chosen individually for your dashboard or any other campaign overview. The dashboard also shows the comparison to last months.

Fully responsive – looks beautiful on all devices. Automatically adapts to desktops, laptops, tablets & smartphones screens. Choose from over 20 statistic or chart elements on your dashboard which you find most important.

Watch Your Most Important Campaign Statistics

Your most crucial campaign numbers are on the top. With one view you can customize up to 10 different campaign numbers. Besides the usual elements, like impressions, clicks, CTR or CPC you can also see average ACoS, average CZT and average sales per day.

You can see your last uploaded campaign data with all relevant, vital data. See statistics for every single campaign or combined numbers. Select any date period within your available data.

See Your Top Performing Campaigns

Top performing campaign shows you what ad campaigns bring you the most sales. Flexible data tables are sortable on each column. Analyze where you spend the most, where you receive the most clicks or impressions, or which ad campaign has the highest CPC.

Set your sales and ad target for each month. Beautiful circle charts show you every day the percentage you have reached so far during the month. All dashboard charts also show the percentage compared to last month in the same period.

Keyword Optimiser – Minimise Ad Spending

With the click of a button, your campaign keywords are analyzed and optimized for better performance and more sales.

Improving your Amazon book campaign performance is now a snap. Simply select a keyword campaign you uploaded and hit the start button. In just a few seconds you get various optimization reports. These can be exported with another click into a new campaign. Furthermore, you can set each optimization parameter individually to match your ad profile (available in the Pro account).

Campaign Split Testing – Know What Works

Choose a time span, select any two campaigns, and see which ad makes you more profit.

Have you ever wondered if all the changes you make to your campaigns pay off? Testing different ads is an important strategy to maximize the effectiveness of your ad campaign. Compare ad text, different pricing, categories, and keyword sets.

There is no other tool currently on the market that provides you with these sophisticated tracking abilities. It is now a breeze to use your campaign data, upload them to the Book Ad Report, and watch in real time how the program turns these numbers into meaningful and delicious looking charts.

You can now finally turn your attention back to scaling up your ads, sell more books and make more money. Tracking is no longer an issue! Check it out below and see the many chart examples on the website.

Here is the link to the Book Ad Report tool: Book Ad Report

Chapter 8 - Troubleshooting

My Ad Got Rejected - What Now?

All ads go through a manual approval process once you submit them. There are usually two aspects that the Amazon team is looking at: the landing page and the ad text that you have used.

Amazon provides only a few of the guidelines that the approval team uses to approve or reject a campaign. Please also see Amazon's Creative Acceptance Policy - a link is provided in the resource section.

You might have already tried to submit a Sponsored product or Product display ad, and it was disapproved. The Amazon answer may sound like this: "Thank you for submitting your campaign. Unfortunately, it was rejected as it doesn't follow Amazon's guidelines. Please check our creative guidelines". When you get this message the first time, you may scratch your head because it does not say anything about the specific reason the ad was disapproved.

Let us look at some of the guidelines that Amazon doesn't provide on their website.[34]

All text must be spelled correctly. ASCII art is not acceptable. Calls to action must be clear and direct. Vague calls to action for example ‚Click now' are not acceptable. Exclamations should not be used unless it is part of the brand/product name.

Using ALL CAPS is not allowed, unless: the title on the detail page is formatted in the same way; it is a brand name; the word is a well-known abbreviation such as DIY (do it yourself).

Not everyone from Amazon's approval team knows and follows their own guidelines.

Superlative statements or claims are not allowed e.g. ‚Best science fiction book on the market'.

- Ad copy must be appropriate for a family audience and cannot contain overt sexuality, words that are vulgar or profane.

- Ad copy cannot denigrate another company or product, for example: ‚better made than [company/brand/named product]' is not allowed.

- Creative cannot include references to the rating, rank, price or specific savings – this is due to dynamic customer ratings, sales ranking, promotions, prices and savings at Amazon.

Use of Awards and Logos

You can use awards and logos in the ad copy if you follow the below guidelines:

- The awards must be present on the product detail page(s) or landing page that you are linking your ad.

- The entity that offered the award must be named.

- All awards and logos must be legible (on mobile as well), and must include the date when the award was won.

The Use of Third-party Reviews

You can use reviews in the ad copy of your campaigns, if they are also verified on the product detail page(s) or landing page that you are linking your ad. You can also add Amazon customer reviews in the ad copy. In this case, you can only add the name of the reviewer if you have received his/her consent. This is to protect the customers' privacy.

It might be difficult for the approval team to identify customer reviews, so if the Amazon team disapproves the campaign, send them the link to the review. They should review the campaign again and approve.

The Use of non-specific Savings, Deals or Discounts

You cannot make price references in the ad copy of your campaigns, as the price is another dynamic element on Amazon, similar to the star ratings.

If you have followed these guidelines and your ads are still rejected, you may want to contact your account manager and ask him to investigate, review, and approve. If you prove to them that you have followed the guidelines, they would normally review again and approve.

My Ad Gets No Impression - What Now?

How long has your ad been running?

If you have no impression on a Sponsored product ad after three days most likely your keywords are the problem. If you are referring to a Product display ad, then you need to wait at least one week, in some cases up to 2-3 weeks until you can determine the next action. Product display ads need much longer to go into the system than Sponsored product ads, which usually show the first impressions after 2-3 days.

If you have not a single impression on a Sponsored product ad after five days, then it is highly likely that you should check the following:

- How many keywords do you have in your campaign?

- How targeted are these keywords?

- How did you get these keywords?

- How did you set the bid price of these keywords?

It would be best if you started your ad campaign with about 50 keywords that are highly targeted to your book. Please reread the chapter on keywords to make sure you are doing things right.

If you have enough keywords, and they are targeted to your book, how frequently are these keywords searched on Amazon? Check some of these keywords with the MerchantWords online tool.

If they are frequently searched in Amazon, then your bid price may be to low. Increase your bids by five cents and check again in a few days. Sometimes it helps to increase the bids to an uneven number e.g. 11/16/21/26/31 cents. I think most people go with even bids like 5/10/15 cents and so on.

If you check all these facts, your ad will get start to get impressions. After that happens, continue to optimize your keywords for this campaign until you reached an optimum amount of impressions.

My Ad Gets No Clicks - What Now?

If you get no clicks at all from your ad campaign then first check the following:

- How long has your ad been running?
- Is your ad targeting the right audience?
- Is your ad text compelling and makes people click?
- Does your book has a professional cover?
- Is your book title interesting to readers?
- Is your price maybe too high?

I could not get a decent statistic on the average click-through rates from KDP advertising. From my experience, it seems it is in the range of 0.1%. This means you should receive on average one click per thousand impressions. If your ad has less than a thousand impressions wait a few days more and check again.

If your ad has received 5000 impressions or more and not one single click, it's time to analyze what probably is going wrong by looking at the possible causes above.

Check the facts above and start either updating your campaign, adding an ad variation or launch an entirely new ad. Experimenting and patience is the key to success here. Advertising on Amazon is not a set and forget approach.

Please note, that when your ad has a very low click-through rate over a longer period, Amazon may terminate it due to bad performance. Most likely your ad targets the wrong audience.

Amazon and other platforms like Google are interested that the ads are relevant to the visitors. If they aren't a visitor or potential buyer gets too much distracted, and they abandon the site.

Google won the search competition by showing more relevant searches to their users. They changed their algorithm years ago already from a ,keyword' based search to a ,meaning' search. They even hired one of the smartest guys - Ray Kurzweil - to build a search engine that works like a brain. You will find some book recommendation in the resource section.

I am Losing Money on Ads - What Now?

When you start advertising with Amazon, it's not unlikely that you may lose money on your ad campaigns. Don't worry too much, and please don't give up and stick around.

Losing money means your ad is working but needs some optimization to get into the green light area.

Please keep in mind that you should wait with optimizing until your campaign has enough clicks generated. If your average keyword has only five clicks than you need to wait a bit longer until you start to optimize and tweak.

Sponsored Product Ads

Depending on what campaign you are running the fix is different. Let's start with the Sponsored product ad using keywords. First, take a look inside the campaign, where you can see all your keywords and the related stats. Now, click twice on the ‚Clicks‘ header to sort this column by ascending. It would be best if you looked at the keywords with the most clicks on top. Look at the Sales and ACoS column.

What you most likely see is that you have several keywords with a right amount of clicks but no sales or just one. As a first step, you may want to pause these keywords and focus on other keywords which give you better ACoS.

Next, you may want to look at keywords that work. That's the ones where the ACoS is below your break-even point. If you don't know how to calculate your break-even point, please re-read ‚Chapter 3 - What is ROI & ACoS?‘. Now, look at the ACPC column and your bid price. If they are very close together, e.g. your ACPC shows 35 cents and your bid is 40 cents, then increase the bid by up to 25%. In our case, the new bid would be 50 cents.

Another option is to look at keywords that perform well and add related keywords. Use MerchantWords to find related keywords that are actually searched by Amazon users.

You can use other tools, for example, Google Ads offers a free keyword planner. You need to sign up for an account to use it. However, don't worry, as long as you don't use Google Ads, you can use this tool for free. Keep in mind that the Google tool does not show you keywords used on Amazon. I mentioned the difference between the Amazon search and the Google search earlier in the book.

After each optimization, allow the ad campaign to run at least another week until you have enough data to make another tweak. By the way, the BookAdReport program offers semi-automatic tools to optimize your campaign. It looks at specific parameters and gives you suggestions where and what to optimize. This is a real time saver because tweaking your ads is time-consuming.

Optimizing Sponsored product ads with automatic targeting is easier, but may take a while until you have reached a positive ACoS. If your ad text is good, and your book cover looks professional, your ad should eventually work. If you lose too much money, lower your bid and give it time. Amazon's algorithm needs time to figure out where to show your ad for optimum sales. This is an automatic process, and the more clicks and sales your ad generates the better Amazon can optimize the placement of your ad.

Once your campaign works and makes money, try to increase the bid in five cents steps and wait at least a week until you can see the difference. You need to look at the stats from the previous week and compare it with the latest stats. That only works if you download your campaign stats. You can use the BookAdReport program to upload your stats on a daily basis. When you do this, you will see the exact difference of your optimization effort.

Product Display Ads

If you have target your ad by ,Interest' you have only one option to optimize your ad. Experiment with a lower and a higher bid price for a week or so and see if that makes a difference.

The next strategy would be to change the interest group. However, that's not an option, because you need to create a new campaign. Amazon does not allow you to change the interest group of a running campaign. So, hit the copy button to duplicate the campaign and only change the interest group. You may want to pause your original campaign or leave it running with a lower or higher bid price to compare it later with the new campaign and the different interest group.

I am Just Brake Even - What Now?

This is a similar scenario as to what we talked before, with the difference that you are not losing money. Never terminate or pause a campaign that just breaks even! Why? Because you get free book exposure, which leads to sales eventually on other campaigns you are running. It may also help your own author website with sales or building a reader interest subscription list.

The optimization methods are basically the same as in the previous chapter. You may also want to look at keywords that get no impressions at all and pause them. Also, look at keywords with high impression numbers and only a few clicks. You may want to pause them as well. The more keywords you have in your campaign that generate sales, the better.

Amazon is interested in showing readers the best matching options. For them to do this, they look at each campaign and generate an internal scale on how they perform.

That's the same strategy Google is using. They want to deliver the best matching results to the user. If they don't do this, the user does not find what they are looking for right away, and the next search engine is just a few clicks away. Again, Google won the Internet search race by delivering the best matches based on linguistic analysis.

Afterword

When I started with advertising on Amazon, I was excited about the opportunity to give my books a sales boost. With millions of books listed on Amazon the chance your book is found is very rare.

The most sales originate from author's websites or any form of social sharing websites like Twitter, Facebook, and Instagram. If you don't write a blog and you don't have a large volume of followers on any social media outlets your choice of marketing your books leads to Amazon.

Amazon ads is not a set and forget model - I wish it would be that easy. It takes a fair amount of time and understanding to be successful with advertising your book on Amazon. Luckily, this is not a black box technology anymore. It is relatively easy to set up your first ad and see some sales happening. When this happens, please congratulate yourself and realize that you just succeeded in marketing your book!

It does not matter if you lose out at the beginning and you are not breaking even with your advertised money and the sales you made. You don't need to spend much money on your Amazon ads. With $50 per month, you can get a decent start and learn a lot about marketing your book.

It takes time and patience to work your way up. However, what you will learn on your way may help you also to open up other channels where you can market your book. Many authors are successful with Facebook ads, and they used what they have learned before with Amazon ads.

I encourage you to stick with it; even you are frustrated and disappointed. Feel free to email me if you have anything interesting to share about your successful campaign or some tricks you discovered.

Also, please let me know if you missed anything in this book that really should be covered. This is the first edition, and I am planning already the second extended version of this book. Your feedback is valuable to me, and I will answer your questions.

Last, but not least please use the tools that I recommended in this book. They will save you much time, help you with important decisions, and they also support you in analyzing your campaigns. At any point in your advertising adventure, you need to know what you are doing, what works and what doesn't. Keep on experimenting and try new things.

Leave Your Review on Amazon

I don't have a publishing contract with one of the five big publishing companies, which have Millions to spend in promoting their books. I am a self-publishing author dedicated to helping people with my 18 financial books, and now with this new essential advertising book.

A lot of sweat and hours of research, combined with over 12 months of testing went in this work. If you found valuable information in this book, please give it a solid 5-star review on Amazon. In case, you don't feel it deserves that, please don't hesitate and write me an email with topics you did not like or maybe missed.

Again, I value your input and I appreciate your honest feedback.

Sincerely

Thomas Herold

Resources

Recommended Websites

Amazon Ads

https://authorblberry.com
https://www.tckpublishing.com/amazon-book-ads/
https://kindlepreneur.com/amazon-ads-case-study/
https://davidgaughran.com/2018/09/19/advertise-sell-more-books/
https://chrismcmullen.com/tag/kdp-ad-campaign/

Self Publishing

https://selfpublishingadvice.org/how-to-choose-the-best-keywords-when-publishing-on-amazon/

Book Formatting / Images

http://www.darcypattison.com/publishing/format-picture-books-kindle/

Book Description

https://www.tckpublishing.com/how-to-write-book-descriptions/

Amazon Advertising

https://advertising.amazon.com/lp/books
https://advertising.amazon.com/ad-specs/en/policy/creative-acceptance
https://services.amazon.com/advertising/faq.html
https://images-na.ssl-images-amazon.com/images/G/01/AdProductsWebsite/downloads/Kindle_Authors_and_Book_Publishers_Creative_Acceptance_Policies.pdf
https://kdp.amazon.com/en_US/help/topic/G200634560

About Amazon

https://www.marketwatch.com/story/how-amazon-came-to-dominate-books-electronics-and-the-cloud-2017-05-12
https://www.britannica.com/topic/Amazoncom
https://www.theatlantic.com/technology/archive/2018/07/amazon-kindle-unlimited-self-publishing/565664/
https://authorlink.com/writing-insights/five-cautionary-points-to-ponder-before-publishing-on-amazon/

Writing Ads

https://www.wordstream.com
http://www.infomarketingblog.com/100-good-advertising-headlines-victor-schwab/
https://www.businessmagazinegainesville.com/the-psychology-of-ads/
https://exploringyourmind.com/psychology-of-advertising/
http://www.media-marketing.com/en/opinion/the-thirteen-most-powerful-words-in-advertising/
https://www.janefriedman.com/using-amazon-kdp-ads-sell-ebook-amazon/

Book Business

https://www.idealog.com/blog/changing-book-business-seems-flowing-downhill-amazon/
https://qz.com/1240924/are-ebooks-dying-or-thriving-the-answer-is-yes/

Book Marketing

https://chrismcmullen.com/2017/11/03/book-marketing-by-the-numbers/
https://theonlineadvertisingguide.com/glossary/click/
https://davidgaughran.com/2018/05/31/marketing-uncovered-how-to-sell-books/
https://www.janefriedman.com/optimizing-books-amazon-keyword-search/
http://nicholaserik.com/start/
https://okdork.com/10-marketing-tactics-to-net-41000-downloads-on-amazon/

https://medium.com/@nkolakowski/amazon-kindle-e-book-marketing-tools-do-they-actually-work-f49bff0e244c
http://www.stevescottsite.com/book-marketing
https://www.locationrebel.com/increase-amazon-kindle-book-sales/
https://www.tckpublishing.com/how-to-become-a-1-bestselling-author-on-amazon/

Promotion Tools

http://kindlebookpromotions.com/
https://kindlepreneur.com/list-sites-promote-free-amazon-books/
https://blog.reedsy.com/book-promotion-services/
https://www.fiverr.com/gigs/kindle-promotion

Video Courses

https://www.udemy.com/book-advertisement-with-amazon-ams/
https://www.udemy.com/how-to-make-market-and-sell-ebooks-all-for-free/
https://www.udemy.com/kindle-marketing/
https://www.udemy.com/amazon-ads/
https://www.udemy.com/ams-ads-for-authors/
https://www.writersonlineworkshops.com/courses/mastering-amazon-for-authors
https://www.tckpublishing.com/fta-video-1

Statstics

https://www.statista.com/topics/1177/book-market/

Audio Books

https://findawayvoices.com/
https://www.acx.com

Author Earnings

http://authorearnings.com/report/january-2018-report-us-online-book-sales-q2-q4-2017/

Tracking Tools & Tips

http://theauthorbiz.com/tracking-data-to-maximize-your-income-with-brian-d-meeks/

https://www.synccentric.com/

https://bookadreport.com/

https://sellics.com/

Keyword Tools

https://www.kdspy.com

https://parsehub.com/

https://www.merchantwords.com/bookadreport

https://www.yasiv.com/

http://sonar-tool.com/us/

https://www.kdprocket.com

Pricing Strategies & Royalties

http://thefutureofink.com/kindle-pricing-strategies/

https://www.davidwogahn.com/kindle-royalties/

http://lindsayburoker.com/e-publishing/pricing-your-ebook-at-99-cent/

https://fixmystory.com/2016/08/18/the-ultimate-guide-to-choosing-the-right-price-for-your-book/

Image Optimization Tools

https://tinypng.com/

https://imagecompressor.com/

https://compressor.io/

Book Cover Art

https://www.canva.com/
http://angelahaddon.com/
https://kindlepreneur.com/book-cover-design/
https://blog.reedsy.com/book-cover-design/
https://en.99designs.de/
https://www.creativindiecovers.com/
https://diybookcovers.com/3Dmockups/

Publishers

https://www.bookbaby.com/
https://www.ingramspark.com/
https://www.fiberead.com

Book Categories

https://www.tckpublishing.com/competitive-amazon-kindle-bestseller-categories/
https://www.goodreads.com/list

Book Reviews

https://www.tckpublishing.com/self-published-professional-book-reviews/
https://www.thekindlebookreview.net/
http://www.kindlebookreview.net/
https://kindlepreneur.com/how-to-get-book-reviews-with-no-blog-no-list-and-no-begging/
http://kindlebookpromotions.com/
http://www.100reviewers.com/
https://www.publishersweekly.com/pw/reviews/index.html
https://www.amzdiscover.com

Other Books By Thomas Herold

The books listed below are all available on Amazon. Most of them in Kindle and Paperback format. Please feel free to check out the author page here.

The Money Deception - What Banks & Governments Don't Want You to Know

Financial Terms Dictionary - Terminology Plain and Simple Explained

Financial Terms Dictionary - Real Estate Terminology Explained

Financial Terms Dictionary - Corporate Finance Principles & Fundamentals

Financial Terms Dictionary - Investment Terminology Explained

Financial Terms Dictionary - Banking Terminology Explained

Financial Terms Dictionary - Principles of Economics Explained

Financial Terms Dictionary - Retirement Planning and Investing Guide

Financial Terms Dictionary - Trading Terminology Explained

Financial Terms Dictionary - Accounting Quick Reference Guide

Financial Terms Dictionary - Acronyms & Abbreviations Explained

Financial Terms Dictionary - Laws & Regulations Explained

Building Wealth with Silver - he Biggest Wealth Transfer in History

The Author's Websites

Book Ad Report. The advertising campaign dashboard you always wanted. Turn your plain amazon book campaigns into significant, delicious charts. See your ad campaign performance over selected time periods at a glance. The only advertise and marketing dashboard for amazon direct publishing authors.

bookadreport.com

Money Deception. Major financial changes are coming – are you prepared? In this new explosive book 'The Money Deception', Mr. Herold provides the most sophisticated insight, and shocking details about the current monetary system. Never before has the massive manipulation of money caused so much despair and economic inequality all over the world.

moneydeception.com

Herold's Financial Dictionary. The most comprehensive financial dictionary with over 1000 financial terms explained. Clear and concise article style description with practical examples.

financial-dictionary.com

The 100 most popular and important financial terms explained. You can get a free copy by going here:

https://www.financial-dictionary.info/free-book/

Bibliography

[1] Statistics and Facts about Amazon - https://www.statista.com/topics/846/amazon/

[2] Amazon by the Numbers - https://wearetop10.com/amazon-stats/

[3] The E-Reader Device Is Dying A Rapid Death - https://justpublishingadvice.com/the-e-reader-device-is-dying-a-rapid-death/

[4] Porter Anderson - Latest from Author Earnings - https://publishingperspectives.com/2016/06/author-earnings-more-data-profitable-authors/

[5] Book Market Statistics & Facts - https://www.statista.com/topics/1177/book-market/

[6] Mahogany Turner-Francis - https://www.bookstr.com/book-genres-that-make-the-most-money

[7] Statista - https://www.statista.com/topics/1488/e-reader/

[8] The Demographics of Device Ownership - http://www.pewinternet.org/2015/10/29/the-demographics-of-device-ownership/

[9] Statista -Audiobooks in the U.S. - Statistics & Facts - https://www.statista.com/topics/3296/audiobooks/

[10] Statista -Leading audiobook genres - https://www.statista.com/statistics/249846/preferred-audiobook-genres-in-the-us/

[11] Statista - https://www.statista.com/statistics/707093/attitude-e-books-cheaper-than-printed-version/

[12] BookBaby - How Much Should You Charge for Your eBook? - http://blog.bookbaby.com/2012/09/how-much-should-you-charge-for-your-ebook/

[13] WrittenWord - Pricing Strategies to Sell More Books and Maximize Author Earnings - https://www.writtenwordmedia.com/2018/07/25/ebook-pricing/

[14] WrittenWord - Pricing Strategies to Sell More Books and Maximize Author Earnings - https://www.writtenwordmedia.com/2018/07/25/ebook-pricing/

[15] Fix My Story Jordan Smith - https://fixmystory.com/2016/08/18/the-ultimate-guide-to-choosing-the-right-price-for-your-book/Jordan Smith

[16] Dave Chaffey - Average display advertising clickthrough rates - https://www.smartinsights.com/internet-advertising/internet-advertising-analytics/display-advertising-clickthrough-rates/

[17] Randy Duermyer - Return on Investment - ROI Defined https://www.thebalancesmb.com/roi-return-on-investment-1794432

[18] Technopedia - Web Scraping - https://www.techopedia.com/definition/5212/web-scraping

[19] Scott Allan - Self Publishing School - https://self-publishingschool.com/more-categories-on-amazon/

[20] Dan Brady - Book Publishing - https://ukbookpublishing.com/unlocking-hidden-ebook-categories-kindle-direct-publishing/

[21] Theresa Ragan - Sales Ranking Chart - https://www.theresaragan.com/salesrankingchart/

[22] Kindlepreneur - Sales Rank Calculator - https://kindlepreneur.com/amazon-kdp-sales-rank-calculator/

[23] Joseph Sugarman - The Adweek Copywriting Handbook - https://www.amazon.com/Adweek-Copywriting-Handbook-Advertising-Copywriters/dp/0470051248

[24] Bunny Blog - How to write great advertising copy in six steps - https://voicebunny.com/blog/how-to-write-great-advertising-copy/

[25] Dan Shewan - 8 Best Ad Copywriting Tips - https://www.wordstream.com/blog/ws/2016/03/14/ppc-ad-copywriting

[26] Dan Shewan - 8 Best Ad Copywriting Tips - https://www.wordstream.com/blog/ws/2016/03/14/ppc-ad-copywriting

[27] Using Numbers in Writing: Tips for Your Print Marketing - https://www.printwand.com/blog/using-numbers-in-writing-tips-for-your-print-marketing

[28] Jill Ferris - 100 Greatest Headlines of All Time -https://www.responsecapture.com/campaign-optimization/100-greatest-headlines-of-all-time/

[29] Una Kostandinovic - The Thirteen Most Powerful Words in Advertising - http://www.media-marketing.com/en/opinion/the-thirteen-most-powerful-words-in-advertising/

[30] Systemagic Productions - Effective Advertising Words - http://systemagicmotives.com

[31] Systemagic Productions - Effective Advertising Words - http://systemagicmotives.com

[32] Scribe - Tucker Max https://scribewriting.com/write-book-description/

33 Scribe - Tucker Max https://scribewriting.com/write-book-description/

34 Dominic Amariei - Ad Copy Guidelines -https://www.amazonppc.com/12-ad-copy-guidelines-that-you-need-to-know-to-get-your-ams-ads-approved/